A
Survival Guide
for
New Consultants

ALVIN ALEXANDER

A Survival Guide for New Consultants

Copyright 2014 Alvin J. Alexander

First edition, published February, 2014

(Previously named, *Zen & The Art of Consulting*)

Table of Contents

"Learn the rules well.
Then forget them."

~ Basho

Introduction

"Act without doing, work without effort."
~ Lao-Tzu

If you think all high-paid consultants are great-looking people who dress impeccably and know the answers to all the problems, I can tell you that's just an illusion.

Myself, I'm not the best looking guy in the world. I wear glasses, I'm at least a little overweight, and my yoga instructor always tells me to stand up straight. I buy my suits off the rack. I'm not an eloquent speaker either. If I give my best attempt at a rousing, "Knute Rockne" speech and then ask you to run through a wall, you probably won't. I'm smart, but my IQ is probably only in the top fifty percent of the world, not the top 5% or 1%. The way I solve problems tends to be a lot more like Peter Falk's Columbo than the brilliant Sherlock Holmes.

But for fifteen years, I was arguably one of the best software consultants in the Louisville, Kentucky area. Louisville isn't well known, but it's the 16th-largest city in the United States. Unlike very expensive cities like Boston or New York, the cost of living in Louisville tends to be below the national average, but even with that low cost of living, my salary as a consultant consistently exceeded $200,000 and even $300,000.

How did I do it?

I don't have one single magic formula or silver bullet, but in this book I'll share a collection of the most important tips I discovered as I learned to become a successful consultant. I'll cover the main topic of "Your Work as a Consultant," along with other major sections on Sales and Marketing. I also started a multimillion dollar consulting firm named Mission Data, so if you're interested in starting your own consulting business, my section on "Building a Consulting Business" provides my best tips to help you start your own business.

Who this book is for

While writing this book, I thought back to the beginning of my own consulting career, and asked, "Would this knowledge have helped me then?" I also thought back to the consultants I hired at Mission Data, and how I unfortunately threw them into the lion's den without any training. I feel comfortable saying that if I had written a training manual back then, this book would be that manual. (More on this shortly.)

I've found that the best consultants are people with ambition, so this book is for them. It's written for the consultant who wants to be involved in the "big decisions," the consultant who meets with clients to discuss their most challenging problems, the consultant who writes sales proposals and project plans, influences decision makers, and has happy, long-term customers. It's for the person who aspires to be a partner in a consulting firm, or wants to run his own consulting business.

Almost twenty years ago I had those same aspirations, but what I didn't have was a blueprint for how to succeed as a consultant. I had to learn from trial and error, and as the saying goes, "Trial and error is a great teacher, but the lessons sure are painful."

Finally, while my own background is as a computer software consultant, almost all of the lessons I share in this book apply to the consulting field in general, so they'll be helpful to business process consultants, project managers, accountants, lawyers, and other service professionals.

My background

I absolutely was *not* born to be a consultant. If you talked to people I went to high school with, they'd probably say something like, "Al? Oh, yeah, he was the guy that didn't speak more than once or twice a semester."

Fortunately for me, some time after high school I began talking to people, eventually getting a degree in Aerospace Engineering, and then working on projects for Department of Defense (DoD) and NASA contractors. After learning the Unix operating system and C programming language while working on my last NASA project, I got tired of the relatively small raises I could make working in the aerospace industry, so I made the leap to become a computer consultant.

I began my consulting career with an existing computer services firm in Louisville, Kentucky in 1993. To do this I had to take a pay cut from (a) over $50,000 a year to (b) a salary of $35,000 plus "incentives." Because I didn't know what it took to be a consultant, and the firm I joined had no idea what to do with someone who knew C and Unix, my incentives were very small, and this pay cut lasted for a long time. But in less than three years -- after working more than ninety hours a week trying to find the right formulas for success -- my income had finally exceeded a rate of $100,000 per year. (Assuming a 4% inflation rate, that's over $200,000 per year in 2012 money.)

In 1995 I left that computer services firm, was forced to sit out a one year "noncompete" agreement, and then founded my own consulting firm, Mission Data, in 1996. Ten years later, after earning salaries in excess of $300,000 per year, I sold that company, which by then had fifteen full-time employees and nearly $2M per year in revenue. (You can read about that sales process in my book, "How I Sold My Business: A Personal Diary.")

Training consultants

While I was running Mission Data, I realized that different employees were saying different things to our clients, in both the sales and consulting processes. While we were fairly consistent in our technical approach, our consultants would often handle "people problems" in different ways, and in some cases, they used approaches that I had tried and failed with during my lean years. Although I didn't want to create a company of robots who would always speak and act in exactly the same way, I wanted my employees to understand my philosophies on how to work with people and succeed as a consultant, so I put together a presentation to discuss the best approaches to consulting.

That presentation eventually became the basis for this book. So although you and I don't have the opportunity to work together, I'm glad to say that the advice I'm sharing in this book is the same advice I would have given you had you worked for me at that time.

About the book format

Although I could easily write hundreds of pages about my consulting experiences, I wanted to create a book that is "accessible," a book you can speed-read over one or two nights if you like, or perhaps read more slowly, focusing on just one chapter at a time. With this format -- and with the extra "Summary" chapters at the end of the book -- you can also use it as a reference, such as the night before a big meeting with a client.

In summary, this book is a collection of more than thirty small chapters that cover over 160 pages in length. I hope you enjoy the stories, and more importantly, I hope that you can use the lessons I learned to make your consulting career incredibly successful.

Section 1: Your Work as a Consultant

My initial plan was to present the sections in this book in the order in which you work with clients: Marketing, Sales, and then Consulting. But because I feel like my greatest strength is as a consultant, I'm beginning this book with a collection of stories that demonstrate what I think it takes to succeed as a working consultant, where you'll be advising clients and providing solutions.

1.1) Where there's mystery, there's money

"What is your original face before you were born?"
~ Zen koan

I don't remember where I heard it first, but possibly the most important phrase I've ever heard related to the consulting field is this:

Where there's mystery, there's money.

When I began my consulting career in 1993, I was fortunate to have learned about the Unix operating system through my work on a NASA project. Back then, understanding Unix was a rare skill, and with things like client/server software gaining popularity -- and the Internet about to explode -- I was in a great situation. Although I didn't yet know how to find customers, I knew Unix, and potential clients needed people who knew Unix -- it was a "mystery" to them.

I could have ridden that wave for a while, but I was more interested in computer programming than being a Unix or network administrator, so I learned about object-oriented programming (OOP) and the Java programming language. Fortunately I had once again had stumbled onto a "mystery," and in the late 1990s and early 2000s you could easily charge $125/hour or more for programming services. Customers only knew that they needed web applications, but *how* to create them was a mystery.

Keep learning

As time went on, knowing Java and OOP wasn't enough. As the industry matured, I needed to learn how to estimate the time and cost of software projects, so I learned something called Function Point Analysis. As my projects got larger, I also had to learn how to run successful software projects (a process a friend refers to as "herding cats"), so I learned about software process management techniques like eXtreme Programming (XP) and Scrum.

As I write this book in 2012, most programmers know about Java, OOP, XP, and Scrum, and in fact they also know about many other things like Test Driven Development (TDD), Behavior Driven Development (BDD), web services, "big data," and much more. In fact, most programmers are now familiar with multiple programming languages, and if you can't write in other languages like Scala, Groovy, Python, Ruby, or PHP, you look like a slacker.

The point of this discussion is that as a consultant, at least as a software consultant, you need to keep looking for the *mystery*. You need to have a feel for where the market is moving, where the next great technology is coming from. If all you know these days is Java and OOP, you're probably still worth something, but not nearly as much as someone who knows some of the specialized technologies I mentioned. If you want to make the big money as a computer programming consultant, you not only need to keep from having your skills become obsolete, you also have to be aware of the cutting edge.

For consultants in other industries this may sound a little extreme, but in the computer industry, there are many stories of companies who were popular one year, and dead the next. For instance, in the early 1990s, a company named Novell sold software that provided the way for building computer networks. But by the end of the decade they were obsolete, wiped out by Microsoft and Cisco. A consultant who made over $100,000 a year by working with Novell products in 1993 was worthless by 1998 -- unless he kept his skills up to date and learned the Microsoft and Cisco tools.

Exceptions to this "mystery" rule?

Are there exceptions to this "mystery" rule? Maybe there are, but I don't know of any. As I think about the different service-oriented professions I know -- web designers, advertising agencies, lawyers, and accountants -- they all have to keep learning.

For instance, because I know relatively little about the artistic part of web design, I'd like to think that great web designers should be set for a long time. You'd think they wouldn't have to learn much because people like me will never be able to break through that "artistic barrier of entry" (a mystery). No matter how hard I try, I'll never be able to make a website look as good as someone with artistic talent. But when I think of what they've had to learn over the years -- from HTML to HTML 5, CSS to CSS 3, JavaScript, DHTML, Flash, etc. -- I know they also need to constantly update their skill set to stay in the mystery.

I've worked with several lawyers and accountants, and you'd think they wouldn't have to worry, businesses will always need their services. But the best lawyer I know told me he always had to learn new case law.

While I'm in the neighborhood of writing about attorneys, I love my tax attorney, and he now charges over $200/hour. But, because he's kept up to date with the latest laws and court decisions, he's saved me money on several occasions. Imagine that: A consultant charges you over $200/hour, but you love the guy and never hesitate to call him because he knows his stuff and can help you save or make money. Now *that* is a good consultant.

1.2) Deserve trust

*"If you cannot find the truth right where you are,
where do you expect to find it?"*
~ Dogen

I've been a successful computer consultant for almost twenty years now, and when people ask me for my secret to success, they're always surprised by what I call "Rule Number One" of consulting:

Deserve trust.

I know that may sound trivial, but it really is the first rule. Let me give you an example, and then you can decide whether you think "deserving trust" should be Rule #1.

A simple example

You've been working for Customer A for a long time now, and every time they asked you a question you've been able to answer it, so you've got a great track record. But today they call you into a meeting, and when you walk into the conference room there are several people you don't know, so the pressure is on.

You answer several questions easily, when suddenly you're hit with a question you don't know the answer to. What do you do? Do you feel the pressure to come up with an answer -- *any* answer -- because all these people are looking at you as the high-paid consultant? I've seen many other consultants do exactly that, and I'm here to tell you, that's absolutely the wrong approach.

As a consultant -- shoot, just as a regular, everyday human being -- if you lie to someone, and they catch you in that lie, you've lost their trust. As you probably know from your own life experiences, it takes a long time to gain someone's trust, and just a moment to lose it.

The correct response

When people ask a question you don't know the answer to, there's a very simple way to reply that builds confidence and trust. All you have to say is something like this:

> "Off the top of my head I don't know, but I'll be glad to research this and get back with you."

This reply shows several important character traits, including honesty, an interest in the problem, and initiative. You're being truthful, and you're also doing what you're supposed to do, being a first class problem-solver.

I could go on for a while with many more stories just like this one, but my guess is that you already knew Consulting Rule Number One. But you may have thought consultants always had to have all the answers at their fingertips, and I can tell you that based on my experience -- and millions of dollars in successful projects -- that isn't the case.

The trick to gaining trust

At the end of this book I'll share the names of a few of my favorite books related to the field of consulting, and just last night I saw the following quote about *trust* in one of those books that summarizes what I just stated:

> "The trick to gaining trust is to have no tricks."

Tell the truth, deserve trust, and you'll gain trust.

Trust gets tested

If all of this sounds trivial to you, here's the abridged version of a story you'll find later in this book: One day I accidentally let a computer virus/worm loose on one of my customer's networks, and it affected *hundreds* of their computers, and probably cost them many thousands of dollars. However, because I had always been honest with them, this didn't ruin our relationship, and in fact, it led to a more open relationship.

1.3) Be a problem solver

"Out of clutter, find simplicity."
~ Albert Einstein

My second major rule to being a successful consultant is also simple:

Be a problem solver.

When I first began to succeed as a computer consultant, it suddenly occurred to me what I was: *A technical hit man.* Seriously. My job could be described like this:

- Customers had technical problems.

- I made the problems go away.

- Customers paid me a lot of money.

You might like that description, or you might not, but that's the way I viewed it in my early days, and that view was only reinforced once I became a small business owner.

Finish the project

In my early days as a computer programmer, back around 1994, I was horrible. On one particular project, I estimated it would take 3-4 months of normal work to complete a project with a client, but it took over five months, with a lot of overtime. The actual cost of the project was more than double what I expected it to be. I thought the client would be furious.

But despite the delay in the project and the high cost, the client was fairly happy, and we continued to work on additional projects. Why were they happy? They told me later it was because *I finished the project*. Where other internal developers and consultants had failed, I had at least shipped the product, and they now had a product they could sell to their customers.

A manager's perspective

Once I became a manager, and later a small business owner, this belief that the most valuable employees make problems go away was reinforced.

If you haven't been a manager before, let me tell you a simple secret:

> Good managers *really* appreciate
> people who get things done.

> (And the faster, the better.)

By definition, a manager has a pile of things to get done, and limited resources he can use to get those things done. In my life as a business owner and manager, if an employee gets work done, that means:

- Our desired tasks are getting done, so

- We are competing as desired against our competition, and

- They're making my life easier, so I can think about other things.

- They'll be well-paid as a result.

Conversely, if an employee keeps bringing me problems without also offering solutions, or they move so slow that the competition beats us, they're making my life harder, and in short, I'm thinking about how I can replace this person with someone else.

So my advice is simple: Think of yourself as a "technical hit man," make problems go away, and you'll be well-paid as a result.

1.4) Keep the peace

*"When you become you, Zen becomes Zen.
When you are you, you see things as they are,
and you become one with your surroundings."*

~ Zen Master Shunryu Suzuki

By now you're a trustworthy person who makes problems go away. What more could a client want?

In my role as a computer software consultant, I'm often paid more than twice the salary my client's programmers make, and I also get to work on the exciting, new projects, while they get to maintain the old stuff. (This is like your spouse hiring someone else to design and plant a beautiful new garden, while you get to cut the grass.) So when I'm working at a client site, an important role for me is to not create any more problems for my sponsor than they've already created by the sheer act of hiring me. (I refer to the individual(s) who hired me as my "sponsor," and I'll use that term here.)

This means the following:

- I dress well. I wear a suit until my sponsor tells me not to. Even then, I usually continue to dress very well. My very real excuse is that I often have to meet with other clients, and while I may be exceeding the dress code at this location, it's often necessary when meeting other clients. (I don't recall anyone ever being fired for dressing well, but I know of several cases where people not meeting a minimum dress code has caused problems for them.)

- I'm not rude to anyone, and in fact, I'm very polite to people who obviously aren't happy that I've been hired.

- I understand my roles on the project, and the roles of other people. If I'm not sure, I ask.

- I understand where my sponsor and project fall within the company's organization chart. If I'm working for the Service Department, I understand that, and when someone from the Sales or Manufacturing Department asks me for something, I'm polite, but say that I'll have to check with my sponsor (the Service Department) and get back with them.

- I offer a variety of "peacekeeping" solutions to my sponsor, such as offering training classes and seminars for the other people on staff.

- I don't go over my sponsor's head. For instance, I don't "cc" people on emails unless my sponsor has told me to. I avoid anything but polite conversation with my sponsor's supervisors. I want the higher-ups to know my name and what I'm doing, but the person who hires me should always get all the credit.

- I keep my workspace clean. If everyone else has a clean workspace, but mine is very dirty, that's a poor reflection on me and my sponsor. At the very least, consider yourself a guest in someone else's house, and act appropriately.

So the first thing you do at a client site is simple: Don't create problems for your sponsor.

Avoid office politics and traps

You also need to avoid office politics and traps. These come in many forms, including:

- A manager of another department may be a "political animal," and they may try to get you involved in their turf wars. I politely decline to help them in their climb up the corporate ladder, and report all incidents to my sponsor.

- Discussions of religion, politics, and even sports may lead to a quick end to your consulting relationship. Avoid them.

- Office gossip. You have no role in office gossip or politics, you're just a visitor. Keep your ears open if you like, but your mouth shut.

- People will come to you with resumes. Sometimes it will be their resume, and they'll want to work for you. Politely say that can't happen, it's in your contract that you can't hire them. Other times it will be the resume of "a friend." In all cases, handle these situations with care.

- There will be times when you're having a bad day, maybe a very bad day. If you're working at a client site, I encourage you to get away from there. Don't dump your problems on your client.

New opportunities

I alluded to this briefly, but while you should never create a problem for your sponsor, you should also keep your eyes and ears open to new opportunities.

In a perfect world you'll solve a problem for Department A, and your sponsor will then refer you for a problem in Department B. While it often works that way, I've also won new business by being aware of new business opportunities at a client location by simply keeping my eyes and ears open, and by making friends.

The funniest (and most profitable) example of this I can recall is when I kept running into a Senior VP in the hallway of a Fortune 500 company. My work had nothing to do with his department, but by the sheer act of constantly running into him in the hallway, we finally had a conversation one day. He stopped me in the hallway and asked who I was, and what I was working on. I introduced myself, and told him what I was working on. He said something like, "You're always smiling and you seem like you're in a hurry, so I had to ask who you are." I told him I'd try to slow down a little, and he said, "That's all right, I like to see it." And then he said with a wink and in a hushed tone, "Keep smiling, people will wonder what you're up to." A few years later I received more than a million dollars in business from this gentleman.

1.5) If you were my brother ...

"The way is not difficult.
Only there must be no wanting,
or not-wanting."

~ Chao-chou

Once you've become the high-paid, top-level consultant you desire to be, an important of your work comes down to giving advice. Once the big decisions have been made, there can also be a ton of detail work to be done -- but it all starts with the big decisions.

In the programming field, the big decisions are known "architecture." For instance, is it better to use Java, Ruby, or a Microsoft or Oracle technology on our current project? How will we handle the massive amounts of data we're looking at? How will we handle redundancy?

In the web design world, the big decisions are "How will we organize the site?", "How will navigation work?", "How do we incorporate the brand?", and so on.

As mentioned, once these big decisions are made, there's still a lot of work to be done, but as Mr. High-Paid Consultant, these are the decisions you'll be involved in on a regular basis, so the question becomes, "How do you become worthy of making those decisions?"

"If you were my own brother ... "

Imagine this: You've just been promoted, and you've finally made it as a high-paid, top-level consultant. You finally get a chance to play with the big boys.

In your new role, you've been working hard on a particular problem, and you have three possible solutions to the problem, A, B, and C, and they're all good solutions. How do you decide which one to recommend to your client?

In the first chapter of this book I wrote that you should be honest, and in this chapter on "giving advice," I'll take this a step further. I highly recommend that when you're considering alternatives and trying to decide on the one right solution, you should consider the client as being your brother, sister, or best friend, and then imagine standing in front of your client and saying these words:

> "Mr. Client, if you were my own brother, I'd recommend ..."

To be clear, I'm not saying you have to use these words when you introduce your solution; I'm saying that when you're trying to decide between solutions A, B, and C for a particular problem, you should think of yourself as giving advice to your brother, sister, or best friend, someone you really care about, and then make your decision. If you then want to use these words in your presentation, that's fine, they're powerful words, but I also recommend not overusing them. If you use them once in a presentation to a specific client that's fine, but if you use them in every presentation, they can easily become overused.

I've found that this way of thinking clarifies my own thought process, and it also helps me sleep at night. By thinking this way, I have complete empathy for my client, and as the words infer, I'm giving them the same advice I'd give if they were a family member.

Advice to my own family

Years ago, during the Christmas of 2008, I ran into a small situation like this with my own family. My nieces wanted (needed) a new computer for Christmas, but they wanted a Windows PC. By that time I had become a Mac user, and in fact I hadn't used a Windows system at all for two years. Although my nieces *thought* they wanted a Windows system, I knew that Microsoft was in the middle of the Windows Vista debacle, and I felt in my heart that Mac OS X was a much better operating system than Windows. Also, because I knew I'd end up being the support guy, I felt like it was important that I gave them something I could support, so in the end I bought them an iMac from Apple.

After some initial skepticism at my decision, I'm glad to say that several years later, they're very happy with the decision I made for them. (I ignored what they thought they wanted, and gave them what I thought was the best thing for them.)

Advice, not fact

Notice from this story that someone else -- maybe a Microsoft employee or Windows network administrator -- would have given their nieces a Windows PC. The point here is that there was no clear factual decision. It's not as clear as having an infection and then having a doctor say, "Take this penicillin, and your problem will absolutely go away." At the time of that decision, Microsoft owned something like 95% of the PC market, while Apple's share was only 5%, so the majority of people in the world would have opposed my decision.

But because I used the two operating systems daily for several years (before finally giving up on Windows), I was in a situation to see what many others could not: In my opinion, Macs were much better than Windows computers at that time. What seemed like a scary decision to my sister and her nieces was an obvious decision to me, so I treated them exactly like what they were, my relatives and friends, and I made the decision for them: "I know you wanted a PC, but in my opinion that would be a mistake, so I bought you this Mac. In the words of Adrian Monk, you'll thank me later." (They did.)

Understand your client's goals

There's one other point to consider here: You can't really understand "the best decision" for your client unless you completely understand their goals.

In the case of my nieces, I knew the most important point was that they needed a computer to do their homework on, and I knew the

Mac would let them do that. Of course they also had secondary goals, such as being able to browse the internet and sync music with their iPods, and I knew the Mac would let them do these things as well. Finally, I also felt that if they used Windows PCs at school and a Mac at home, they'd be better off for that experience.

Summary

In summary, you should (a) know your client's goals, (b) treat them as you'd treat your best friend, and (c) make your decision.

1.6) Learn how to influence people

If you've read the previous chapters, you're now well past the basics. You're a trustworthy person, a problem solver, you don't create any problems for your sponsor, and you know how to make the big decisions. Now we'll dig into a few of the finer points of being a consultant.

At this point, perhaps the most important thing you can learn is how to influence people.

Influencing people

In a perfect world, your work as a consultant goes something like this:

1. You're hired to solve a problem.

2. You investigate the problem, and come up with a solution.

3. You share the solution with the client (you "sell" the solution).

4. You implement the solution.

5. The client is happy.

If you were a doctor, the first three steps of this process would be described this way:

1. A patient comes in with a problem.

2. You diagnose the problem.

3. You prescribe a cure for the problem, i.e., some "medicine."

Unfortunately every once in a while you'll run into a problem in Step 3 of this process where your client will refuse to take the medicine. You can run into this problem for a variety of reasons, including:

1. The client doesn't understand you.

2. You didn't fully understand the problem.

3. The client doesn't trust you.

4. You're not a convincing presenter.

5. All other reasons.

I tend to be a confident person when I'm prescribing the cure in Step 3, and I also tend to fully explain the cure when I propose it, so I don't run into the "client refuses to take the medicine" problem very often, but it still does happen. When it happens to me, my problems are almost always #1 and #2: Either I didn't explain my solution well (most common for me), or for one reason or another I didn't fully understand the problem. I haven't run into #3 in a long time, and #5 is a beast all of its own that gets into things like office politics, turf wars, technology wars, etc. What I'd like to focus on in this chapter is #4, "You're not a convincing presenter."

Um, er ...

One of the smartest technical people I've ever known was a horrible presenter. Even though he was almost always right on technical matters, people rarely accepted his ideas when he made his presentations. If I presented his suggestions it was usually a done deal, but if he presented them, it was always a battle to get the work approved.

The only differences I'm aware of in our presentation styles are:

1. I rehearsed my presentations. I made sure I led the client from (a) where we were, to (b) where we wanted to be.

2. Whatever the subject matter, I knew how I wanted the presentation to end. (In general, I wanted my ideas to be approved.)

3. Because I rehearsed my presentation, and knew what I thought was best, I was confident.

4. Because I practiced, I didn't use filler words like "um," "er," and so on. (I beat myself up when I rehearse and use words like this.)

5. My presentations took less than half the time of his.

Every difference in our presentations goes back to the fact that I rehearse what I'm going to say, and as a result, I'm confident when I say it.

Learning to speak well

Learning how to speak well and with confidence is an incredibly important trait for a consultant. By simply planning what you want from a meeting, rehearsing the subject matter until you know it cold, and then speaking it as planned, you will succeed.

The only way to get better with any form of public speaking is to practice, practice, practice. The good news is that over time this gets much easier.

My "flop sweat" experience

If it helps to know it, while I feel very comfortable speaking these days, I had the dreaded "flop sweat" experience with one of my earliest presentations. I was twenty-four years old, working in the aerospace industry, and working for a small business, and the owner of that small business hated giving presentations. As a result, although I knew nothing about a particular subject, he forced me to go to California with him and give a presentation to the Board of Directors of a multibillion dollar aerospace corporation.

It was the most humbling experience of my life. While I tried to prepare, I just couldn't learn the material fast enough, and my presentation was a humiliating flop. During the presentation the perspiration started, and it just wouldn't stop. I wished people would quit looking at me, but they wouldn't. I kept turning to look at the wall where my slides were projected just so I could wipe the sweat off my face. By the time I was done, my shirt was soaked, and I was humiliated.

I try not to blame other people for my problems, but in this situation -- because of his own fear of public speaking -- my boss put me in a position to fail that day, and I certainly did. For a time I considered doing something else for a living, until I realized that I had been set up for failure by someone else.

A later success

I almost immediately quit that company, and just eighteen months later a second supervisor put me in a situation I could win. I was working on a project for a NASA subcontractor, and once a year we had to give formal presentations of what we were working on to the primary contractor, NASA officials, and other government officials.

Despite my earlier flop sweat experience, I was still very ambitious, and I wanted to make more money than a NASA subcontractor could pay me. My supervisor knew this, so he asked me to help him out and give a presentation on a very controversial topic before I left. I agreed, but I confided with him about my earlier disaster, and told him I didn't know if I was up to the task. To get ready for the big test, he helped me prepare my presentation, made sure I knew all the subject matter, and made me rehearse in front of my peers before giving the presentation to the people at NASA.

At the beginning of both the rehearsal presentation and the actual presentation, my heart was pounding and my throat was dry, but I didn't sweat. After a few minutes and a few deep breaths, I was able to calm down, and I was eventually able to use my nervousness to make a more energetic and forceful presentation. As I gave the real presentation, I realized I really did know the subject matter, and I knew what I wanted to say. Not only could I talk confidently about the current slide, I was able to think ahead and make a smooth transition to the next slide.

In short, my presentation was a success. After the presentation, people I didn't know came up to shake my hand. My boss had a big smile on his face. A few friends at the company congratulated me, saying I had opened some minds on a very controversial topic. With this success, I knew I was ready to begin my career as a consultant.

While that presentation was a resounding success, what might really amaze you is that within a year I was giving presentations to more than 150 people at a time -- and I was anxious to increase that number to five hundred or more people! Less than three years after my embarrassing flop sweat disaster, I was ready to speak in front of anyone who would listen.

Lessons from an automotive service rep

As I write this chapter, I'm sitting in a Toyota dealership, having some service work done on my car. One service department representative here is an outstanding communicator, really terrific at influencing customers. He speaks in a direct, matter of fact manner, and is confident in what he says. When speaking to some people sitting next to me, he approached them like this:

> "Mr. and Mrs. Smith, we haven't been able to find anything wrong with the tires or suspension system, so I recommend that we rotate and balance the tires to see if that eliminates the vibration problem you're feeling. If you have the time, we can do this in less than thirty minutes, and it will cost $X. Would you like to proceed with this plan?"

Notice that there isn't anything magical or poetic in his words, he just spoke in a very clear manner, stating that they can't find a cause for the problem (what we'd call a "bug report" in the computer industry), but despite that, he suggested a possible plan of attack to resolve the complaint.

As an employer, I appreciate what he did. Not only did he offer a problem, he also offered a potential solution. A lesser employee might have only said something like, "We can't find the problem. What would you like to do?", or perhaps, "We can't find the problem. Why don't you take the car back and see if it gets worse or becomes repeatable?"

I say this all the time, but a good employee never presents a problem without a possible solution. People who know me have heard the phrase, "You get ten points for finding the problem, and ninety points for solving it." That's what I really appreciate about this service representative. He acted as a consultant with these people, saying, "We don't know exactly what's wrong, but if you want to try to solve this problem today, it's our professional opinion that this is the next, best step to take."

Getting people to take action

In the book, "The Secrets of Consulting," Gerald Weinberg offers a great quote and story about influencing people. Here's the quote:

> "You can make buffalo go anywhere you want, just
> as long as they want to go there."

According to his story, buffalo will run right through a barbed wire fence, so the only way you can "control" them is by making your desired destination more attractive to them than the alternative.

This is similar to a much earlier quote from Dale Carnegie:

> "There is only one way under high heaven to get
> anybody to do anything. Just one way. And that is
> by making the other person *want* to do it."

In his excellent book, "How I Raised Myself From Failure to Success in Selling," Frank Bettger shares that quote, along with this one:

> "The most important secret of salesmanship is to
> find out what the other fellow wants, then help him
> find the best way to get it."

As I've mentioned, what most clients want is for a problem to go away -- they want a solution to their problem -- so if you've worked diligently and you're convinced that you have the best solution, selling it should be easy: Just tell them why it's the best approach.

1.7) A simple secret to running a great meeting

"When I enter the interview room,
I vow with all beings to trust my innate gumption
and simply say it or do it."

~ Zen Master Robert Aitken

As a consultant, you're expected to run a professional business meeting. In the few minutes before a meeting starts you can be as nice as you want, ask your client how his kids are doing and so on, but once the meeting starts it should be as quick and efficient as possible.

The "secret" to making a meeting snappy is very simple:

> Know what you want out of the meeting before it starts.

When you go into a meeting that you're running, you should know exactly what you want out of the meeting. For instance, when I play the role of a Business Analyst who's designing a software system, my focus is on only three things:

1. I want to know the requirements for the software.
2. I want to design the database.
3. I want to design the user interface.

Because I know I have these larger goals, I often walk into a specific meeting with the thought, "In today's meeting we're going to finish the Order Entry portion of the database design." Furthermore, because I know this is what I want, I send out a meeting invitation well beforehand, stating this specific goal, and I supply any materials I think the meeting participants will need. Once the meeting begins, I keep it focused only on the Order Entry database.

In other meetings you may play the role of salesperson or sales consultant, where the end goal of the meeting is to walk out with a signed sales agreement. As a result, you should have a contract prepared and ready for a signature, and you should be prepared to handle any final objections and close the deal.

Although he wasn't necessarily talking about meetings, Stephen Covey said it very well:

> Begin with the end in mind.

Organization before the meeting

As I mentioned, a great way to run a meeting is to send out a document beforehand that states the meeting's purpose and agenda. You may not be able to do this for sales meetings, but for technical meetings this approach leaves no excuse for people being unprepared, and it also lets decision makers know whether they need to be at the meeting, or not.

Ironically, in some cases I've found that being this organized leads to meetings being canceled, but that's okay, too. Had the meeting gone on, it would have been a waste of time, and by the sheer act of your being organized, you've saved your client and their employees time and money.

Assume control

I take this next point for granted, but I often see young consultants make this mistake, so it's worth mentioning here:

> You called the meeting, and you know what information you need. You invited the participants, and they agreed to come. Therefore, it's your meeting, and even if you're twenty-five years old and everyone else is much older and more experienced than you are, it's still your meeting, don't let anyone else run it. Period.

When the meeting starts, hand out printed copies of your agenda, and then say something like this: "As you know, I called this meeting because we need more information about X, Y, and Z. Item X is the first item on the agenda, and here's what I think about it." At that point you present your ideas and ask your questions, but even when other people are speaking, always remember, this is your meeting, and you're responsible for keeping it under control. If they get off track, it's your responsibility to bring them back on track.

Keep it moving

As people move up in the business world, they have more and more responsibilities, and less free time. Therefore, they appreciate a well-run meeting. Conversely, I've seen more than one executive go ballistic at a poorly run meeting. (Not my meetings, thank you.)

As a result, whenever I call a meeting, I keep it moving. If someone starts to get off track, I bring them right back to the purpose of our gathering.

I can recall many meetings where technical people who rank low on the corporate ladder have started arguments about trivial details, when the purpose of my meeting was a high-end discussion that included executives of that same client. When this happens, I put a gentle but firm end to that argument by saying something like, "That's very interesting, but the purpose of this meeting is to discuss XYZ, so we'll talk about that later. Getting back to the second item of our agenda, let's discuss Option A." The executives at the meeting will appreciate your ability to control the meeting, while also not slapping down their employees.

Other meetings will seem funny (or sad)

Once you learn how to properly run a meeting, the "funny" thing is that when you later go to a poorly organized meeting you'll find yourself laughing (or crying) about the vagueness and apparent lack of purpose of the meeting. I often find myself wondering, "Why are we here? What is the purpose of this meeting?" When you find yourself thinking about other meetings this way, you'll be well on your way to running better meetings yourself.

On a related note, here's a quick tip on dealing with poorly run meetings: If you find yourself trapped in a poorly run meeting, find a polite way to get out of there. If the meeting started at 2pm and was supposed to last an hour, but 3pm is rapidly approaching with no end in sight, let everyone know you have to leave: "Guys, I hate to do this, but I planned on this meeting ending at 3pm, and I promised I'd write up my TPS report by 4pm. I'm sorry, but I'll have to leave at 3pm on the nose." When you do this, you'll be amazed that most people rapidly get back on track, and suddenly manage to finish the meeting by 3pm.

Close it up

At the end of a meeting, you should (a) summarize the results of the meeting, and (b) assign action items. You summarize the meeting to make sure everyone agrees with your conclusions, and you assign action items so everyone knows what to do next, and who is doing what. If you close a meeting like this, people will be impressed and realize you mean business.

1.8) Be good at what you do

"Chop wood, carry water."

~ Zen saying

This point seems obvious, and I hesitate to mention it, but if you want to be an excellent consultant, you should be good at what you do. To be clear, I'm not saying that you have to be great, but you certainly should be good. (Put another way, how can you possibly provide competent advice to others unless you're good?)

For instance, in my opinion, *most* people that come straight out of college aren't ready to be a great consultant. In the computer programming field, no matter how good you are as a programmer, you just won't have the experience you need to be a great overall consultant. That being said, I do think that if you have the talent and ambition, you can be a terrific *apprentice*, and you should try to find a good consultant you can learn from.

Just as I don't think most people straight out of college are ready to be a great consultant, if you're not in the top 25% of your craft, you probably shouldn't be a consultant. Maybe large consulting firms can get away with hiring average people, but if you want to work on your own as a consultant, or work at a small consulting firm, you have to be really good. Period. At least in the software industry, people will test you, and if you can't pass their tests, you won't get hired.

How do you know if you're good?

I suspect most people know if they're any good, but if you don't, just look at your yearly reviews and see what they say about you. In my own history, I was getting 10-15% raises in the aerospace industry when others were being laid off, and my last performance review before starting Mission Data said, "Al, you are a freaking machine. Keep it up!"

You should also be getting excellent raises. Before I was a consultant, my salary almost doubled in my first four years out of college, increasing from $29K to $55K. If you're only getting cost of living raises, you're probably not meant to be a consultant.

You will be tested

As I mentioned, if you're trying to sell your services as a consultant, you will be tested. In the software world you may be tested during your initial meetings with prospects, where they bring along one or more of their gurus to drill into your head to see what you're made of. Or it may happen later on, after you're on the job, and other developers come over to quiz you. If you're not good, word about your lack of skills will get around fast, I can assure you of that. And sooner or later it will get around to the people that hired you.

While these sorts of "tests" may primarily happen to people in the computer and engineering fields, I suspect they happen to some extent in every field. For instance, I never hired an accountant or lawyer without grilling them about what they knew about the computer consulting industry and small businesses. If they gave me direct answers I hired them, and if they didn't, I didn't.

Keep your skills up to date (training)

If you combine this chapter with my earlier chapter about "Where there's mystery, there's money," you should see the need to continually train yourself on the latest products and technologies, and the importance of finding ways to test yourself.

As a consultant in the field of software development, I've had people ask me hundreds of questions over the years, from basic things about the Java programming language, to object-oriented programming, the Unified Modeling Language (UML), cost estimating, Function Point Analysis (FPA), CSS, JavaScript, DHTML, Spring, Hibernate, and many, many more programming-related questions.

As I wrote earlier, you don't need to know all the answers, but you should know many of them, and you should also be very aware of the state of the art in your industry. For instance, I haven't done very much with this tool called Hibernate, but I have played with it, and I know the basics of how it works. I've also read many articles of what's good about it and what's bad (the proverbial "lessons learned"), so I'm not a total newbie. For this particular toolset, that's all I care to know right now -- I don't need to use it on any current projects -- but there are other tools I do know much more deeply.

It has also been my experience that your clients and coworkers will really like it when you share some of this knowledge with them. You can say something as simple as "Wow, have you done any work with RMI yet? It's so cool." For me, this form of sharing is fun, and it encourages them to share with you, and importantly, not be intimidated by you. From a business perspective, it's also a good way of building goodwill with others, and it never hurts to have some goodwill on your side.

Tolerating a beast

Finally, if none of those other points convince you, I will say that I have seen customers suffer along with a consultant, even when the consultant is a total jerk, just because the consultant is good at what they do. Of course they git rid of him as soon as they can do without him, but they'll usually tolerate him when they need his expertise.

1.9) You can't always save the client

"When you can do nothing, what can you do?"

~ Zen koan

As I've mentioned, you're hired to be a consultant because you're a problem-solver, so it really hurts when you can't help a client. It's a tough lesson, but it's an important one:

Despite your best efforts, you can't always save the client.

From what I've seen, you can run into cases that are similar to what I've heard about alcoholics or drug addicts: You can't help someone who doesn't want to be helped.

On one of my strangest projects, the solution to the problem was clear, and in fact, it was incredibly obvious. If the customer just did X, Y, and Z, the problem would be solved, they would likely save *millions* of dollars compared to alternate approaches, and they would rapidly be in a position to provide a great service to their clients before their competitors could react. But they didn't take my advice, and in fact, they were fairly rude about not taking it.

Unusual behavior

Their behavior was so contradictory to "normal" behavior I thought surely they must be a mole in the company, planted there by a competitor to help sink them. But no matter what I tried, they refused to go with the obvious solution, and eventually went down another path. I don't know exactly what they did, because I essentially resigned from the position. (Technically my contract was up for renewal, and I told them I wasn't interested in renewing it.) I told them I couldn't agree with their decision, and they would have to go down the path they chose by themselves.

I resigned from the position for several reasons. First, I wanted to protect my reputation. I thought the "solution" they wanted was so wrong that they would surely fail, and I didn't want to be any part of it. If I stayed on the project they'd be able to walk around the company and say, "Al's on board with our decision," and I just couldn't let that happen.

Second, while I wouldn't go over their heads to upper management to say that I thought they were making a terrible mistake, I hoped that my resignation would become known to upper management, and they would ask me what happened. (People in upper management had known me for years, and I had a good reputation with them.)

Unfortunately the people in upper management didn't learn about (or notice) my resignation until a year later, when, as expected, the project crashed and burned, and millions of dollars had been wasted. The project was suspended, the people running the project were fired, and they eventually implemented my proposed solution, but not until they had fallen behind their competitors.

How I failed on this project

As I look back on this project years later, I wonder if I could have worked harder to influence these people, but I also know that there were other "political" things going on behind that scenes that made it an impossible situation for me to win.

From what I've learned, the lead person on this project held a grudge against me related to an earlier project, and although I always suspected he didn't like me much, and I had been warned that he was hard to work with, I didn't even know I had beaten him out on that earlier project.

I did know that I had to influence this person to get my solution implemented, and I certainly tried. I gave him my information before I gave it to anyone else, to let him sell himself on it, and then present it to others as his own idea. But despite every technique I've ever learned to influence people, this was a battle I couldn't win.

In the end, the only way I could "win" in this situation was to resign and let him hang himself, and that's what happened. This brings up one more important point:

He who documents, wins.

When all the poop hit the fan a year later, my recommendations were "discovered," and I was called back into the company by senior management, and they implemented the obvious solution.

Relationships with senior management

This led to a very interesting discussion with the people I knew in senior management, in which they suggested I should have come to them with my complaints before I resigned. I told them I was very uncomfortable doing that, and if I had done it, it would have made working with this person intolerable.

After a lengthy discussion, they told me that in the future, I should come to them directly if I ever thought there was a problem of this magnitude. They made it clear that my relationship was with *them*, and there was nothing more important to them than they ongoing profitability of their company.

The situation of working with a midlevel manager has not occurred again with this client or any other, but I've always thought that if it does come up again, and my relationship is with people in senior management, I'll seek them out at the start of a project, share this story, and ask them what they want to know if this situation happens again.

The "Can't save the client" pattern

If there's a pattern to this problem where you can't save a client, it usually goes as this story went:

- You investigate the problem and recommend a good solution.

- The client rejects your solution, typically for an unknown reason.

I wish I knew a great answer to this problem -- and I will share one possible technique later in the "Sales" section of this book -- but I've come to accept that there are times you just can't save the client. Some times all you can do is ask the client why they won't implement your proposed solution, and do your best to tell them why you think your solution is the best approach.

1.10) More consulting tips

When it comes to your work as a consultant, working directly with your clients to understand and solve their problems, the preceding chapters contain the most important lessons I know. In this final chapter of the "Consulting" section of this book, I'll share a few brief discussions about a few other important lessons.

Seek first to understand, then be understood

When I was a younger, hotshot consultant (who didn't really deserve to be called a consultant), I often made bad decisions or said stupid things because I didn't understand everything there was to understand about a problem and a solution. For instance, I told one client that they should clearly be using a Unix system instead of the IBM System/360 they were using, because Unix was clearly superior. The only problems with my assertions were (a) the person I said this to was the System/360 administrator at the company, and (b) the software they used to run their company only ran on the System/360. That was the last day I worked with that client.

I encourage you to listen to your client's problems, make notes, and repeat your understanding of their problems and goals back to them before attempting to offer any sort of solution.

Learn to assess people quickly

When meeting people for the first time, either in a sales meeting or in a project meeting where you're meeting new people, learn to assess people quickly. In sales meetings, ask yourself, "Who's the *real* decision maker here?" Very often it's not the senior person.

In all meetings, keep an eye out for how people behave, and try to "feel" if people are:

- Can-do, get it done people
- Big talking, no-action types

- Passive, "I wish I was somewhere else" types
- Someone who is friendly to you
- Someone who is unfriendly
- Someone who seems to have questions or concerns

The people with unspoken questions or concerns may sink you later, after the meeting, so I recommend always asking something like, "Are there any other questions?", and then looking around the room, specifically looking at the person (or people) you're concerned about.

Beyond those generalizations, keep an eye out for people's:

- Strengths
- Weaknesses
- Hot buttons

"Hot buttons" are especially important in the sales process, which we'll discuss in the Sales section of this book.

Under-promise, over-deliver

It's very important to deliver what you say when you say you can get it done. If you say, "I'll get it to you by Friday," deliver it on Friday. Better yet, deliver it Thursday. The first important thing here is that someone may be counting on you to deliver it at that time, and if you don't, you're creating a problem for your sponsor. (You're just one link in a larger chain, and you just broke the chain.) The second important point here is that you're building trust in your relationship; you're delivering what you say you can deliver.

Don't waste time

As I've mentioned before, don't waste time, especially your client's time. If you're "on the clock," billing by the hour, keep it moving. I once had a customer tell me a long joke while I was working, almost ten minutes long. When he finished telling his joke, he suddenly said something like, "Oh crap, that joke just cost me $50, didn't it?"

Regardless of what people say, they're at least subtly aware that you charge for your time.

Best practices and lessons learned

In the software industry I've found that the best managers want to know about things like "best practices" and "lessons learned." They're always looking for ways to improve. Keep an eye out for the best practices in your industry, and share what you learn with your clients.

Understand business

When I was a hotshot young consultant, I was pretty good technically, but I knew very little about business. You can get away with this early on, but I recommend learning about all things business, things like invoices, AR, AP, and SWOT analyses in marketing. As a problem solver, you'll also find some interesting charts and thought tools in the "Six Sigma" world, and standard ways of representing flowcharts and business processes in the Unified Modeling Language (UML).

Keep it positive

When I grew up, my dad wasn't exactly the most positive person in the world. Rather than build me up, he was more of a drill sergeant, and it was his way or the highway. As a result, I ended up reading books from Zig Ziglar and others to help improve my own attitude. In his books, Mr. Ziglar wrote something I found to be very true, which I'll paraphrase here:

> People who are successful don't like to associate with people with bad attitudes.

It sounds a little corny now, but he said that people with negative, *can't-do* attitudes suffered from a bad case of "Stinkin' thinkin'" and a "Hardening of the attitudes," and I've found that to be true.

When you deal with clients who have climbed the corporate ladder to become successful, or built their own businesses, you're dealing with people who have conquered a lot of odds and obstacles, and I can assure you, most of them have positive, *can-do* attitudes, and if you're a Gloomy Gus who constantly speaks in negative terms, or brings up problems without also offering solutions, these people will avoid you.

As an exercise to improve your own attitude, I strongly recommend paying attention to what you say, and when you say something negative, make a mental note, or better yet, make a note in a notebook of whatever it was you said. Once you start paying attention to what you say, you'll be amazed at some of the things that come out of your mouth.

Don't talk about clients in public

As a final point, even if your contract allows it, don't ever talk about clients in public. You never know who's friends with who, or who might be listening.

As I wrote in my book, *How I Sold My Business: A Personal Diary*, I won a deal that was worth several hundred thousand dollars because I overheard a loud-mouthed, drunken competitor bragging about a deal he thought he had won. Until I heard him talk about that deal, I didn't even know about that potential client. I have several other stories where we "found" new prospects because of similar situations.

Section 2: Selling Your Services

Unlike some people, I draw a pretty clear line between "sales" and "marketing." To me, *marketing* is everything you do to attract the attention of new prospects, while *sales* is what you do when you meet those prospects. Therefore, marketing involves things like radio advertisements, mailers, web pages, Twitter and Facebook posts, seminars, etc., while sales involves face to face discussions with prospects about your services.

This section of the book is about *sales*, the act of selling your services.

My favorite book on sales

Note: Rather than repeat myself throughout this section of this book, I'll try to just make this recommendation once here:

> Buy a copy of the book, *How I Raised Myself From Failure to Success in Selling*, by Frank Bettger.

It's an old book that's probably out of print by now, but go find it, and buy it.

My entire sales career is based on the advice in that very straightforward and excellent book, and almost everything in this section can probably be traced back to this book. If you were my own brother or sister, I'd tell you this same thing: His notes on enthusiasm, trust, asking questions, influencing people, keeping records make this book worth $50, $100, or much more. Think of it this way: If you went to college, what did you pay for one class? In my opinion, this book is worth much more to your career as a consultant than any college course.

2.1) Who do you buy from?

I'll start this Sales section of the book just as I started the Consulting section: In my opinion, the most important part of sales is *trust*. If you're trying to sell me something, especially a service, the first question in my mind is, "Do I trust this person?"

Before reading any further, think about the people you've bought a service from before:

- Automobile repair service

- Real estate broker

- An accountant or lawyer

- A person who mowed your lawn or shoveled your snow

Whenever you bought a service like this before, who did you buy from? *Why* did you buy from them? Did you like them before the sale? What about after the service?

Important qualities

I've found that the people I've enjoyed buying products and services from had these qualities:

- Honesty

- Enthusiasm

- Happy and polite

- Problem solver

- They seemed interested in my problem

- They didn't over-promise
- They could demonstrate past successes, and/or were recommended by a friend

All of these qualities lead to a feeling of "trust." I trust people with these traits.

Trust is an important feeling to me. When my wife and I had a house built, we intentionally didn't work with architects and builders we didn't trust. Some didn't seem honest, making almost sensational promises. Others seemed to have no enthusiasm at all. Another seemed distracted, and didn't respond well to questions or changes we proposed. When I hired lawyers and accountants as a small business owner, there were several people I didn't hire because I didn't trust them for similar reasons. I don't know a thing about cars, but I do the same thing with auto repair shops; if I don't trust the people I interact with, I don't do business with them.

Brains aren't the most important factor

Notice a very important thing I didn't say here:

> I *didn't* say that you have to be
> the smartest person in the world.

Of course it helps to be smart, but that's not how people judge you when you first meet them. (The first things they'll judge you on is your appearance and how you greet them.) Odds are, they're coming to you for a service they don't understand very well, so it's going to be hard for them to tell if you're smarter than a competitor.

For instance, I can't necessarily tell if one accountant is *really* better than another, but I can tell from his answers if he's paying attention to my questions, and has experience with situations like mine.

An excellent tip from Ben Franklin

If you want to be a great salesperson or sales assistant, I strongly encourage you to cultivate the attributes mentioned in this chapter. One way to do this is to follow an approach recommended hundreds of years ago by Ben Franklin, one of the founding fathers of the United States:

> Focus solely on one attribute you want to develop for one week at a time. The next week, focus solely on another attribute.

For instance, in Week 1, you should focus on *honesty*. Be honest in all your interactions, and if you fail to be honest in some situation, ask yourself why you weren't honest, and make a note of it. Don't worry about the other attributes, just spend 100% of your time focusing on being honest in all situations.

In Week 2, focus on *enthusiasm*. During this week, don't let anyone you meet be more enthusiastic than you are. Wake up every morning like you were shot out of a cannon, and keep going like that all day.

Continue this practice for each personality trait you want to cultivate. If you don't like my attributes, look up Mr. Franklin's suggestions and use them. He came up with thirteen attributes that were important to him, and he did just what I said, focusing on one attribute for a full week, then moving on to another. By having thirteen attributes, he was able to cycle through the attributes four times each year (fifty-two weeks), and that worked well for him.

I can't recommend this approach highly enough. It's a tremendous way to focus your mind, and build your character.

2.2) Be a Buyer's Assistant

"When you listen to someone,
you should give up all your preconceived ideas
and your subjective opinions;
you should just listen to him,
just observe what his way is."

~ Zen Master Shunryu Suzuki

As Mr. Bettger writes, a terrific way to think about the process of selling is to imagine yourself as an assistant to the buyer. Imagine that you're on the payroll of your prospect's company, and your job title is "Buyer's Assistant." It's your job to understand your company's needs, and then try to understand how the person you're talking to can help your company. If you can put yourself in your prospect's shoes like this, selling becomes easy.

Empathy

As a consultant, I never considered my technical skills to be my strongest suit. I like to think I'm very good, but I also know I'm not the best technical person in the world.

I always thought my superpower was *empathy*. In many cases I felt like I cared more for my client's problems than they cared about themselves. While some of them worked 9-to-5, Monday through Friday, I felt consumed by their problem, and often worked sixty hours or more per week until the project was done.

When you have empathy like this during the sales process, you become a Buyer's Assistant, and when you really immerse yourself in this role, you'll feel extremely confident in your recommendations, and your customers will be amazed that you've thought so deeply about their situation.

Show your interest

A typical sales presentation for me goes something like this: "Mr. Customer, I've done some research on your company, and I see you sell X, Y, and Z. From what I can see, X seems to be your leading product, is that right? I'm sure I don't understand your situation completely, but assuming that I'm close, I have some initial ideas I'd like to run past you. Would you be interested in hearing them?"

Of course what I actually say varies tremendously according to the client's business, but that's a fairly typical introduction. I've shown that I know who the prospect is, I've done my research, I have an interest in their business, and I might be a problem solver. When you first meet a prospect, it's hard to do much better than that.

2.3) Tell your story

"Without any intentional, fancy way of adjusting yourself, to express yourself as you are is the most important thing."

~ Zen Master Shunryu Suzuki

Assuming that you work for yourself or a small consulting firm, when you first meet a prospect, you'll eventually have to tell a little story about your business. You'll definitely need to talk about the services you provide, and hopefully you can share some success stories. You should also highlight anything that makes your company different from the competition.

The important point here is that you should be prepared to tell the story of your business and service. Just like any other public presentation, you shouldn't make this stuff up on the fly. It's a presentation, and it should be well rehearsed.

At Mission Data, my story was very simple, and went like this: "I got a degree in Aerospace Engineering from Texas A&M University, and after working on DoD and NASA projects, I realized that I loved computing. I moved to Kentucky in 1993, worked for another consulting firm for three years, and then started Mission Data in 1996 to focus on software development." At that point I'd talk about the advantages of our firm, the people we hired, and other projects I thought were relevant to the current prospect. (As a funny side story, I intentionally never told people *why* I moved to Kentucky, and to a person they almost always asked why. This was a method I used to see if they were really listening.)

If your company is involved in your local community, I recommend saying something about that. For instance, we used to offer free seminars on the newest programming techniques, so I often told prospects about those, and invited them to an upcoming seminar if we had one planned. Can you imagine why I thought this was a good idea? If so, take a few moments to jot down your reasons.

2.4) A questioning technique

"Let me have your view as to the reason of birth and death."

~ D.T. Suzuki

Did you see how I ended that last chapter? I intentionally ended it with a question, a question that hopefully inspired you to think a little bit, and write down your thoughts.

What's so powerful about that? The cool thing about this approach is that you own those thoughts. *You* came up with them, *you* wrote them down, I didn't. All I did was ask you a simple question, and the odds are that you came up with the same answers I could have told you.

When you ask questions and let your prospects and clients answer them, you're doing the exact same thing, you're letting them sell themselves.

A $250,000 sale

In my book, *How I Sold My Business: A Personal Diary*, I told the story of how I made one six-figure sale after it looked like we had lost the deal. The short story is that I had the flu, and was laying in bed at home when my business partner called and told me we had lost a large sale to a competitor. However, he added that our prospect had not signed a contract with our competitor yet, and he thought he could still get our prospect to meet at lunch today, if I could make it.

The prospect agreed to the lunch meeting and I got myself out of bed (heavily medicated). I actually knew very little of the project we were bidding on, but as our prospect described the project, and why she was going to go with our competitor, I realized that she thought the most important part of the project was "A", when in reality it was "B." Item A would cost about $50K, and both of our companies were very good at it, but Item B would cost about $200K, and we were clearly superior in this area.

Rather than saying that to the prospect directly, I used this questioning technique to let her talk herself into going with our company. I said things like, "As my partner has told you, I've been sick lately, and don't know all the details of your project. I know the overall budget is about $250K, is that right? And how much of that is for Item A? And Item B? So Item B is much larger than Item A, and if Item B doesn't work, Item A doesn't matter, isn't that correct? Do you know who will be working on Item B if you awarded us the project? And what about our competitor?" I continued to ask questions in this way until the prospect convinced herself that we were the best consulting firm to go with on this project. She didn't give us the project right there at the restaurant, but she called my partner within two hours to tell him she was awarding us the project.

2.5) Objections (and hidden objections)

Dogen-zenji said,
"When you say something to someone he may not accept it,
but do not try to make him understand it intellectually.
Do not argue with him;
just listen to his objections until he himself
finds something wrong with them."

~ Zen Master Shunryu Suzuki

When I wrote about being a Buyer's Assistant, I mentioned that you need to be prepared. In this chapter I'd like to take that a step further, and say that you should be prepared for battle. I don't mean "battle" in a negative, argumentative context, but just that you should be prepared to handle objections.

Despite all your preparations as a Buyer's Assistant, prospects may still raise objections, and you need to be prepared to handle them. They'll say things like, "I like what I'm hearing, but I think your price is too high," or "I'm not ready to make a decision today," and so on.

Going into a very important meeting

One the most difficult meetings I had was with the CEO of our largest client after the dot-com bubble burst in the year 2000. One day during this time, this CEO called and asked if my business partner and I would come into his office the next day. We assumed the news wouldn't be good, so we tried to prepare for the worst.

This CEO was a tall, intimidating man, and sure enough, as soon as we sat down he began telling us of the horrors of the economy, and how he was going to lay off many of his own people, and in regard to us, he was going to have to cut our work in half.

We let him go on talking until he was finished, and when he seemed to be done saying all he had to say, my partner said exactly the right thing. Right at that moment, without any hesitation, my business partner dropped the following on this CEO:

"I hear what you're saying, but you don't need to cut our budget in half -- you need to double it!"

After dropping that bombshell, he continued. "Al here is too nice to tell you the horror stories about the people he works with here every day, but I'm not. I don't have to work with your employees, so I'll tell you what I hear our people saying about some of the people on your staff."

"What I hear is that you've got some people who just aren't getting it, they're not making the transition to the new technologies. They may be good AS/400 programmers, but when it comes to Java and the internet, they're just not getting it fast enough. And if you let most of our developers go, all you'll have left are these people who don't know what they're doing yet, and you're not going to be able to deliver your projects."

The CEO's response

To say the least, the CEO was floored. He sat there with an astonished look on his face for quite a while before he could think of something to say. Finally he regained a little composure, looked at me and said, "Al, is this true?"

I just replied, "Yes, it is."

After a few more moments of silence, he did the most amazing thing I've ever seen a CEO do. In the middle of the burst of the dot-com bubble -- not ten minutes after he was ready to cut our budget in half -- he asked, "How much money do we need to budget for you for the rest of the year?"

Fortunately, we were again prepared, so we were able to tell him how many of our people we needed to achieve his business goals. I don't recall if we doubled our budget exactly or not, but after he laid off a large percentage of his staff, our budget was increased greatly, and we continued to work with this client for many more years.

Lessons learned

My lessons learned from this brief meeting -- I'm sure it lasted less than forty-five minutes -- are as follows:

1) Always be prepared when you go into a meeting. If you don't know what the meeting is about, remember the motto, "Be prepared for the worst, and hope for the best."

2) Be firm. Even when the client says he needs to cut your budget in half, you need to be able to say, "No, I think you need to double it, and here's why."

3) Know how you want the meeting to end, have everything set up for it to end that way, and imagine it ending that way, in success for you. It was great that we could tell our client that he needed to double our budget, but following up that grandiose statement with very specific information about how to solve his business problems provided the power behind the punch.

4) We acted as a Buyer's Assistant. If you rationally looked at what was really best for this business and this CEO, our approach made sense. We didn't lie when we said his people weren't getting it; that was the truth, they weren't. So in our opinion, if he had any hope of delivering the software he wanted to deliver, he was going to have to go with us, developers who knew what we were doing, and release the employees who weren't getting it. If he did what he planned and kept his own people, I'm sure they wouldn't have been able to come close to meeting their deadlines.

Handling hidden objections

Not only do you need to be able to handle the objections a prospect *tells* you, as Mr. Bettger would tell you, there may be another objection you're *not* being told about.

As you find out in life, there are *spoken* reasons people will give when explaining why they did something, and then there are the *actual* reasons they did that thing, and they're often completely different. Mr. Bettger quotes a gentleman named J. Pierpont Morgan, Sr., who said:

> "A man generally has two reasons for doing a thing
> -- one that sounds good, and a *real* one."

In the sales world we refer to these as *hidden* objections, and Mr. Bettger suggests handling these with a simple statement:

> "In addition to that ..."

For instance, when a client brings up an objection that doesn't seem to make any sense, or if you suspect something else is going on, you might ask a question like this:

> "Joe, in addition to that, isn't there something else
> in the back of your mind? Some other reason you're
> hesitant?"

I can tell you from personal experience that I've used this technique, and it works. For some psychological reason we all have hidden reasons for the things we do, and if your prospect is really interested in your product or service, this can be a way to draw them out. In my experience, sometimes people will immediately tell you the real reason, and other times they'll tell you the real reason hours or days later.

2.6) If you just don't like selling

"When the soul becomes the warrior,
all fear melts, as the snowflake that falls upon your hand."

~ From the Kung Fu tv series

Many people tell me they just don't like selling. To that, the first thing I say is, "Don't think of it as selling. Be the Buyer's Assistant, and help them see the right purchase. If your service is the right purchase, you'll know it, and if you're service isn't exactly right, you'll know that too, and following everything I've said in this book, you'll be honest about that assessment."

I've followed this process myself: "Mr. Customer, I have no problems saying I can handle X and Y; I've done things like them before, and I assure you I can get them done. However, I need to be up front and tell you that I'm not 100% sure about Z. I've done things similar to Z before, but your situation is a little different, and I'm going to have to do some research. That being said, I'm confident in my abilities, and I think I can tackle it."

I've never lost business by being honest like this. I may lose a deal in the short term, but I've always had people come back to me later for other business, and I assume that's because I'm honest with them about what I can currently do, and what I may not be able to do yet. (I never say I *can't* do something, because I'm confident in my abilities, and I've always been able to learn anything I needed to learn.)

You're selling more often than you think

If you still think you don't like selling, consider this:

You're probably selling something every day.

Here are a few examples:

- You ask a person for a date
- You try to convince a spouse, partner, or friend to go to your favorite restaurant, or to go see a movie they might not want to see
- You sell a colleague on an approach to a problem
- You sell your house or car
- You sell yourself on getting out of bed on days you'd rather just sleep in
- You apply for a job
- You ask for a raise

If you think about it, I'm sure you can find many other examples of how you sell something almost every day.

You're selling a great product

Some salespeople have a really crappy job. Can you imagine selling used cars when you know there's something wrong with them? I couldn't live with myself that way.

I'd much rather have a job selling something I thought was great, a really terrific product that I believed in with my heart and soul.

Well, guess what? In consulting you're doing just that: You're selling yourself, your own skills.

If you think your skills are good, selling yourself should be easy, a joy. You're not selling crappy used cars, you're selling a terrific product you know inside and out, a product you have complete control over. You know what it can do, and what it can't do currently. There's no reason to lie, you just state the facts, "Mr. Customer, here's what this product can do for you."

Summary

In summary:

- Whether you've noticed it or not, you're selling something every day.

- If you always act as a Buyer's Assistant, you can know in your heart that you're acting in the buyer's best interest.

- In consulting, you have the opportunity to sell a terrific product that you have complete control over -- you!

2.7) Contractual matters

"The moment you start seeing life as non-serious,
a playfulness, all the burden in your heart disappears."

~ Osho

To run a consulting business you'll need a few simple business service contracts to make sales, but I can't really provide those for you here. You can get those from your lawyer, or from some of the legal dot-com websites that are available these days.

My advice to you on these contracts is to keep them short. Our shortest legal agreement was two pages long, and our longest agreement was six pages long. We started with a boilerplate agreement from our attorney, then edited it so we could understand it and easily explain it to our customers.

The other important points I'll say about these sales agreements are:

1. You should list your hourly rate, estimated number of hours, and overall estimate within the agreement. For instance, I might estimate that a project will require 1,000 hours, my billing rate is $125/hour, and therefore the overall estimate is $125,000.

2. You should provide some description of the services to be rendered, such as, "This estimate is to build the XYZ application for Acme Corporation. The XYZ application has been defined in the separate document, 'The XYZ Application Design.'"

3. At the end of the document you should have signature lines for your client and for yourself.

4. You should present the sales agreement to your client, walk them through each page of the agreement, and when you get to the last page of the agreement, hand them a pen and show them where they need to sign.

While an agreement like this may seem daunting if you're just starting your own business, I can assure you that you can usually get them from your lawyer, a legal website, or an appropriate business book at your local bookstore.

2.8) More sales tips

The most important thing I can tell you about selling is to put down this book, and go buy a copy of *How I Raised Myself From Failure to Success in Selling*, by Frank Bettger. It's the single most important book on selling I have ever read.

In addition to that suggestion, here are a few other important sales tips I know.

See the people

As Mr. Bettger writes, when you first start out, sales is a number's game. If you need to see one hundred people to make five sales, then by all means get out there and meet one hundred people. As a way to make sure you're really "seeing the people," keep written records of the people you talk to. The records will initially give you goals to achieve, and later give you confidence, and serve as a database of information that you can use to learn what works best for you. With modern software like Salesforce.com and others, this is easier than ever.

Be enthusiastic

Probably the most important attribute of a good salesperson is that they are enthusiastic about their product. They can share their enthusiasm about their product, and because enthusiasm is contagious, prospects become enthusiastic -- and become clients.

In the first chapter of his book, Mr. Bettger shares several stories about how a *lack* of enthusiasm in his own life almost ruined his baseball career, and later almost ruined his sales career. This is truly one of the best chapters on selling I've ever read.

In sales, I've found that enthusiasm can be like a game, and I get upset when someone seems more enthusiastic than I do. "Darn," I think, "this client is more enthusiastic than I am, I need to kick it up a notch."

Assume the sale

The best salespeople I know always follow the practice of *assuming the sale*. They assume that at the end of the sales meeting the customer will be ready to buy, so they have a contract typed up and ready for a signature.

The process is simple: You go through a meeting, make your presentation, show the client how you're going to solve their problems, then have a piece of paper ready to be signed. "Mr. Customer, as you've seen, our proposal is $10,000 for this solution, and I've taken the liberty to write this up, as you can see here." You hand them a piece of paper and a pen, and show them where to sign.

It doesn't always work that easily, but you'd be amazed if I told you how many salespeople went into a meeting without having something a customer can sign. Don't be timid like that, you're just wasting time -- Assume the close!

What's your budget?

Going all the way from simple sales lessons to an advanced lesson ... the best salesperson I've ever known was excellent at doing something called "qualifying" prospects.

I discuss this in my book, *How I Sold My Business: A Personal Diary*, but in short, you'll get a surprising number of calls from people who don't actually have a budget, or otherwise can't afford your services. (In fact, as I edit this book in April, 2012, I just had one of these calls last night.)

When you first start your consulting business you may want to meet as many prospects as you can just for the practice of the meetings, but once you're successful, you'll want to *qualify* your prospects to make sure you don't waste your time. A terrific and simple way to do this is to ask the simple question, "What is your budget for this project?" You'll often find that the people you're talking to have no idea what the project might cost, or that they don't even have authority to spend their company's money.

What to give away

One of the hardest parts about consulting is trying to decide what to give away during your first sales meetings with prospects. When I'm "on the clock" with paying clients I'll tell them anything I know, but when you're "off the clock" in a sales meeting with a new prospect, this is a delicate situation. You want to earn their business and prove your worth, but you also don't want to give away the solution.

My personal advice is that you give away what you think you need to give away to win the deal … without giving away the solution. For instance, if a prospect is really pushing me to give them answers about solving their architectural problems, I might draw some diagrams on a whiteboard showing what I've done in similar situations for other clients, but if they keep pushing me to solve their problem, I'll finally say something like, "Guys, that's what I get paid to do. Beyond that, I won't claim to understand your complete problem in the short time we've had together in this meeting."

Gerald Weinberg said this very well in one of his books:

"If they didn't hire you, don't solve their problem."

I can recall that twice in my career prospects that didn't hire me called me later to complain about a "solution" I discussed. I had to kindly tell them they didn't hire me, and therefore I have no idea how they interpreted or implemented what I said.

In general, when I really needed clients in my early days (1993 to 1994), I gave away more information during sales meetings with prospects. During my later years I still approached their problems with zeal, but I gave away less information during those sales meetings.

As a final tip here, because I had a business partner at Mission Data who handled most of the sales work (while I played a role I called "sales engineer"), I could let him cut me off whenever I started giving away too much information. He could play the "Bad cop," and say what I mentioned earlier, "Mr. Prospect, we get paid to answer detailed questions like these. If you'd like to sign this contract now, we can get started on that."

Section 3: Marketing

When it comes to the overall set of skills that define "consulting," *marketing* is my weakest topic, which is the main reason it's the third section of this book instead of the first.

Marketing is a little bit of a weakness for me because I was fortunate to start working for one consulting firm in Louisville, Kentucky in 1993, where I made a number of important contacts. When I later started my own consulting firm in 1996, I got back in touch with a few of these clients, and eventually did millions of dollars of business with them.

In part, I was able to initially make these contacts because the firm I joined had an established base of customers and four full-time salespeople. But, because they didn't know anything about the Unix operating system or C programming, those were just starting points for me.

After leaving that firm I had to live out a one-year noncompete agreement, and during that year I worked as a regular employee at a Fortune 500 company. Although I'm horrible at networking, and I was a little burned out at that time and just felt like sitting in a cubicle while I lived out the terms of my noncompete agreement, I forced myself to get out most days and meet new people at this company. I eventually met the CIO, CEO, and several VP's of the company, and when I later started my own consulting firm, these contacts eventually led to more than a million dollars in consulting fees.

As a result of all of these experiences I developed a simple marketing philosophy:

> Once people get to know me, they've always been happy to do business with me. Therefore, I just need to find ways for people to get to know me.

Given that introduction, here are a few marketing techniques I've learned over the last twenty years.

3.1) Your best advertising

*"When the work is done and one's name is distinguished,
to withdraw into obscurity is the way of heaven."*

~ Lao-Tzu

If you're good at what you do (programmer, designer, lawyer, accountant, etc.), by far your best advertising is satisfied customers. I've received millions of dollars of income as a consultant because I solved problems for one client, and that client was kind enough to either hire me again, refer me to another business, or serve as a reference.

Of course this is a Catch-22 situation: You have to have at least one customer in order for this technique to work. But with the assumption that you do have at least one customer ...

Don't be afraid to ask

Assuming your project has gone well, don't be afraid to ask your customer for more work, or if they can refer you to anyone else. "Mr. Customer, it looks like we're going to wrap up this project soon, so I thought I'd ask if you have any other projects I can assist you with?"

If your work is good, this will usually end up one of four ways. First, the client will have another project for you. Second, they won't have a new project for you, but they'll refer you to someone else at the company who may have a project for you. Third, there may be no other work for you at this company at this time, but they may have a friend at another company who might need your help.

The fourth thing that can happen -- and this hasn't happened to me too often -- is that they won't know of any additional work for you *right now*. But even then you've planted a seed. In one case I can recall where a client didn't have any additional work for me, and then sent me an email within a week saying that I should talk to Bob at Acme Corporation, she was sure he'd have a project for me.

3.2) Your second-best form of advertising

"When you meet a master swordsman,
show him your sword.
When you meet a man who is not a poet,
do not show him your poem."

~ Lin-Chi

If you believe what I believe -- that if people know you, they'll hire you -- the next obvious thing is to give new people a chance to get to know you.

Full books have been written about how to find good prospects, but here's a short list of my favorite techniques:

1. Offer free or low-cost seminars relevant to your industry. These establish your credibility, and let you meet prospects in a low-stress environment. (It's low-stress for them, if not for you.)

2. Send postcards to prospects introducing your business. Your postcards should give them some reason to call you, such as a low introductory rate, or a few hours for free. (As I've written elsewhere in this book, I once gave away two days of work at no cost -- and earned million dollars of business in return.)

3. Volunteer in your community. I've always enjoyed working as a volunteer, and as a nice side benefit, I've also met other business owners and even politicians at charitable events. Volunteering can be good for your heart, and your wallet.

4. Work the internet. Create a decent website, and learn about things like SEO and SEM so prospects will find your website. Even if a Google AdSense ad costs $5 per click, that's a lot cheaper than things like radio advertising. (We paid as much as $30,000/year for radio advertising.) Work other internet resources, such as Twitter, Facebook, and LinkedIn. I know from my own experience that this works; although I now live

in Colorado, I still get calls from people in Alaska who have found my old website.

5. Try advertising in trade magazines or local newspapers and magazines.

6. Hire a PR person. My business partner and I got into the Louisville newspaper and local trade journals several times after hiring a PR person and paying her less than $5,000.

My favorite thing about this part of marketing is that this is where the creative aspect of your business comes into play. For instance, if you decide to send out postcards, both the design of your card and what you say is entirely up you.

Note: At this point I highly recommend buying two books from Robert Bly. The first book is titled *Selling Your Services*, and it talks in depth about this extremely important topic of finding new prospects. The second book is titled *The Copywriter's Handbook*, and it discusses how to write text ("copy") that demands attention. If the idea of sending mailers to prospects appeals to you, these are the two best books I know about this subject.

3.3) Make your phone ring

"Zen is not some kind of excitement,
but concentration on our usual, everyday routine."

~ Zen Master Shunryu Suzuki

As a continuation of the previous topic, the most powerful thing you can do in marketing your consulting business is this:

Get customers to come to you.

Cold-calling is bad business

Imagine this situation: You're sitting there at work, and someone calls and says, "Hi, my name is Fred, and I'd like to sell you my services." Personally, I *hate* receiving those kind of unsolicited calls. They make me want to *never* do business with that person.

Cold-calling on prospects has all sorts of problems and barriers:

1. The prospect may not need your service.
2. You may have interrupted something they were working on.
3. Even if they'll listen to you, you have to sell yourself from scratch.
4. As in my case, you may have just lost a potential customer for life.
5. A million other problems ...

Now, if you flip this situation, and get prospects to call you:

1. You know they're interested in your service.
2. More than that, they're interested in your service *right now*.

3. They called you, you didn't call them, so the selling process becomes much easier. They're already "sold" enough to call you.

I could go on for a while, but I think you'll agree that having prospects call you is a much more powerful technique than attempting to cold-call them. For techniques to get prospects to call you, please see the previous chapter.

3.4) How to sell a service

"What is the color of the wind?"

~ Zen koan

In his excellent book, *Selling Your Services*, Robert Bly makes the argument that selling a service is hard because you aren't selling something *tangible* that a prospect can see. For instance, if someone goes to buy a car, they can see a car that they like for one reason or another, and they often become very attached to that tangible thing they want. It may be a muscle car, a gas-saving electric car, a big 4x4 pickup truck, or the color of the vehicle. Whatever it is, it's tangible, something the prospect can see and feel.

Services, on the other hand, are *intangible*. A prospect can't walk into your office, see the attributes of your previous successes, and want to buy them because they're red or blue or fast. Therefore, what you have to do is convert your services into something that is tangible.

Create a portfolio

In general, the way I do this is to create a portfolio of my previous project successes. This includes:

- Stories of each success, highlighting the gains to the client. A simple Problem/Solution format works very well here: "Customer A came to me with this problem; I designed this solution for them, and it met or exceeded their expectations."

- Because I work in the software industry I also create (a) architectural diagrams, and (b) screenshots from applications I've created. Architectural diagrams show my ability to think about big problems, and screenshots show my ability to create decent-looking applications.

- References from former clients. I'm actually horrible with this -- particularly because a few clients can keep me busy for 5-10 years -- but whenever you finish a project and your client is pleased, get a letter of reference from them. Fortunately, these days clients often send you emails saying things like, "You did a great job on my project, I'm very pleased," and you can just ask a client if you can use that text in your marketing material. I've used that technique many times.

Without a portfolio, a meeting with a new prospect involves 100% talking by you to explain what you've done, but when you're working *with* a portfolio, you talk much, much less, and simply explain the benefits you've provided for previous clients, occasionally pointing at some of the nice pictures you've put together to highlight the important features of your successes.

3.5) Sell the sizzle, not the steak

*"One day Chao-chou fell in the snow, and called out,
'Help me! Help me!'
A monk came and lay down beside him.
Chao-chou got up and walked away."*

~ Zen koan

I don't remember where I learned this next technique, but I've never forgotten it:

Sell the sizzle, not the steak.

What this means is that if you're marketing something like beef or a steak, you don't sell the fact that beef has protein, or that you eat it with a fork and knife. Instead, you sell the "sizzle." You mention the smell of the steak cooking on the grill, the smoke coming off the grill, the sizzling sound, perhaps how your beef cuts so easily that it's like a warm knife through butter, or how a cookout can be a great time with friends. The important thing is that in all of these scenarios you're selling *emotions*.

How this works

As I've mentioned several times in this book, I think of myself as a problem-solver, a technical hit-man, I make problems go away. You can therefore say that I sell solutions. But many prospects don't even care about that, they want something more, so I sell *happiness*. I get prospects to think about what their life will be like when the problem that has been bothering them goes away.

For instance, on a recent project, my client was a man who was only a few years from retirement. I was referred to him by someone else I had worked with in the same company, and as we spoke, he told me about a problem with his current software systems. They were frequently failing, and because he ran a 24x7 manufacturing operation, he was getting phone calls at all hours of the day and night, including weekends. He spoke very little about the technical problems, but spoke a lot about being woken up in the middle of the night, having to drive into work, make a few small changes, then do something like reboot a server to get everything working again. The problem was driving him crazy, and his current programming staff couldn't seem to fix the problem.

As he spoke, I once again felt like a technical hit-man: He was desperate to get this problem to go away. Yes, he wanted a solution, but deeper than that, he wanted happiness, peace of mind, and a good night's sleep.

It's important to note here that during our conversation, he probably spoke 80% of the time, while I spoke only 20% of the time. For the most part, probably because I had been referred to him, all I had to do was listen. In this case I didn't really sell my services with emotion -- but only because I didn't have to! His situation had been a problem for so long, all I had to do was to listen to his emotion.

In the end, the problem was difficult, but I solved it, and when he thanked me at the end of the project, it was one of the most memorable moments of my career. Yes, he and his company paid me plenty of money, but his happiness at being able to sleep at night was the thing I'll never forget.

3.6) What's your brand?

"My legacy, what will it be?
Flowers in the spring,
the cuckoo in the summer,
and the crimson maples of autumn."

~ Ryokan

When you own a business, you'll eventually think about the question, "What is my brand?" That is, when people think of your business, what do you want them to think?

The brand at every software company I've run is this:

- We solve problems, often very large, very difficult problems.
- In the process of solving these problems we also provide great customer service.
- If we *seem* to be a little more expensive than others, we're certainly worth it, we always get our man. For instance, we might estimate that a project will cost $100,000, and a competitor says they can do it for $75,000. But if we have historically always solved problems and come in under budget, and the competitor has a less successful history -- meaning they may *not* actually solve the problem -- which price is really higher?

However you want to phrase it, I think of my brand like this:

> My service might *seem* more expensive than my
> competitors, but I always get my man, a little
> something like Sherlock Holmes. In the process, I
> also communicate very well with my client, constantly
> keeping them up to date.

Because I know this is my brand, I make sure that all of my marketing material follows this brand. I make sure that my website and all of my printed material look good, and beyond that, on those days when I don't feel like communicating with a client about a certain problem, I force myself to do it anyway, because I want this to continue to be my brand.

Before you move on to the next chapter, I encourage you to take a few moments and think about these questions: "What is my brand? Am I Mercedes? Porsche? Ford? Toyota? Am I always faster than others? Am I always successful? Do I cost more, or less, than my competition?"

3.7) Who are your customers?

"The fundamental delusion of humanity
is to suppose that I am here,
and you are out there."

~ Yasutani Roshi

I didn't know this when I first started working as a consultant, but I've always had very specific target customers. For instance, I tend to work on large projects, where the smallest project might cost a client $50,000, and a large project will cost several million dollars. Therefore, my clients must generate enough revenue (profit, actually) to be able to afford these prices.

So, even though I love things like ice cream and wouldn't mind spending a lot of time in an ice cream parlor, it doesn't make sense for me to spend a single minute targeting ice cream stores in my advertising: They can't afford me. I need clients who have problems that will cost at least $50K.

As you can imagine, there are many other ways to classify potential clients. A divorce lawyer won't have any need to advertise to businesses. A business accountant may not work on personal taxes. A real estate agent who sells million-dollar homes will have a limited audience.

Market to your target customers

Once you know who your target customers are, you'll have a much better feel for your marketing approach. When I opened my small consulting business in Alaska, I was able to easily find information about potential clients based on my "ideal customer." I got lists from the Chamber of Commerce and other sources, whittled the list of potential clients to about 100 companies, and I targeted those companies with postcards and other forms of advertising. While I eventually had to move back to the "Lower 48" for family reasons, I received enough feedback from those prospects to be very happy with my efforts. (In fact, they continue to contact me even though I now live in Colorado.)

In essence, I maximized my advertising dollars by spending wisely. I didn't waste time trying to market to people who couldn't afford my services.

Understand why customers hire you

A related part of this discussion is that you need to understand *why* people hire you.

If you provide a business accounting service, that may be easy to understand: Small businesses need accountants, but they can't afford to hire them full time, so they typically have one or more bookkeepers on staff, then hire an accounting consultant on a part-time basis to make sure their books are correct, especially at the end of year and tax time.

When I provide a computer programming service, I know people hire me for these reasons:

1. Smaller organizations may have no programming expertise at all, but they need to have custom software written to help run their business.

2. Larger organizations have existing programming expertise, but they may not have enough people on staff to handle new projects.

3. Larger organizations may have programming expertise, but they may not have the specialized expertise I offer. For instance, right now I now how to write in a new programming language named Scala, and I can also write apps for the Android platform. These are new technologies that some programming staffs may not be able to handle.

This seems like basic knowledge to me now, but when I first started in the consulting business I had no idea why people hired me, I was just glad to have some work. Fortunately I learned this lesson before I went broke.

3.8) Networking

"Grasshopper, know yourself,
and never fear thus to be naked to the eyes of others.
Yet know that man so often masks himself."

~ From the Kung Fu tv series

I'm a technical person. I was trained as an Aerospace Engineer, and taught myself to be a computer programmer and systems architect. I don't really like small talk. I'm not a networker. I don't like networking at all. I don't even like the word "networking."

But if you're going to be a consultant, some form of networking is probably necessary. (I say, "probably," because once your company grows, you can hire salespeople, and they seem to like networking more, and at the very least give you someone to go to networking events with.)

The best advice I can give about networking is this:

1. Go to events you think you might enjoy. Most geeks say they don't like networking, but if you get a bunch of Ruby programmers together in a room to talk about the best features of the Ruby programming language, not only will they talk to each other, they'll probably have some lively conversations. (Conversely, if you put them in a room to talk about The Biggest Loser or Project Runway, very few of them will say a word.)

2. Go to events with other people. After starting my own consulting firm I went to many parties in the two weeks leading up to the Kentucky Derby, and I always took a salesperson or coworker with me.

3. Learn how to introduce yourself. In my younger years I was always "Al" or "Al Alexander," but once I began working as a

consultant I found it easier to pronounce my name as "Alvin Alexander," following that with, "Just call me Al."

4. Make sure you know why you're going to an event. If you're a Drupal programmer and you go to an event about Drupal programming, you're probably going to meet other Drupal programmers -- not customers. Therefore, if your purpose is to get more business, you have to ask yourself, "Is it worth going to this event?" The answer may be "yes" if you think other people have Drupal programming work to give you (where you'll be a subcontractor), or the answer may be "no" if you're hoping to run into the CEO of a medium size business who can afford your services. (If the answer is "maybe," go to the event, and find out for yourself.)

5. Learn to like people. That may be a weird sentence for most people, but because I'm not a very social person by nature, networking is hard for me. The one thing I learned after selling Mission Data and traveling around the world is that at least 95% of the people in the world are very nice, and if you just treat them like "long lost brothers and sisters you're meeting for the first time," networking becomes much easier.

6. Rehearse your "elevator pitch." If you know what you're going to say beforehand, it's much easier to say it when you feel a little pressure. Most introductions at networking events go like this:

You run into someone and say, "Hi, my name is Alvin Alexander."

"Hi Alvin. I'm Fred Flintstone. I work with Bedrock Corporation. What do you do?"

"I own a software consulting firm named Valley Programming. We specialize in XYZ. Tell me about Bedrock Corporation."

If you can just get some words out like that to start an

introduction, I find that everything is pretty smooth after that. The biggest questions you need to be able to answer are, "What do you do?", and "Why would my firm hire you?" If you can answer those questions concisely, and treat people like long lost brothers and sisters, the process of networking will be much less painful, and you might just meet some people you like. (If you still have problems talking to people, remember to ask the "W" questions: Who, what, when, where, and why, such as "*What* did you think about that point the speaker made about ABC?")

I don't like networking, but I do enjoy volunteering for services in my community, so this is a simple form of networking for me. I show up for some sort of volunteer work, I do the work, meet nice people, and talk to them while I work. I didn't start volunteering like this to meet business people, but to my pleasant surprise I've met many business owners and several politicians, so it ends up being a form of networking. Of course it's not as direct a form of networking as going to a local Chamber of Commerce meeting, but at least I enjoy it.

Section 4: Building a Consulting Business

In this section I share a few additional stories that I first wrote after selling my consulting firm in 2007. These stories are generally related to the topic of starting and running your own consulting business.

4.1) How I started my consulting career

"The beginner's mind should never be lost."

~ Zen Master Shunryu Suzuki

If you're a new consultant thinking about going to work for a small consulting company, I'd like to share what I went through in the first three years of my consulting life, in particular my thought process about the revenue I was trying to generate. Hopefully there are some valuable lessons in what I went through way back then.

1) Bill enough to pay for yourself

When I first started to work for a small consulting firm in Louisville in 1993, my thought process was very simple: By the end of the first year, I wanted to be billing clients at a rate that was at least as much as I was getting paid.

To keep this simple, let's say your employer is paying you $50K per year to work as a consultant. In that case, Step 1 is to make sure you bill your customers at least $50K per year. To be very clear, when I say, "bill," I mean that invoices are going out the door for work you've performed, and the yearly total of those invoices equals or exceeds your salary, in this case, $50K.

In my case this was very hard. I came to Louisville as a Unix systems administrator and a C programmer, and Louisville was a Microsoft town, and the company I joined was a Novell reseller. So I was essentially starting my own "business within a business," and times were tough. The salespeople at the firm didn't know how to sell my services, and I wasn't much help to them.

2) Bill enough to generate a profit

After a while we found some small customers, and I got to that point where, on a monthly basis, I was billing enough to cover my base salary, and I felt pretty good. Then I learned the important lesson that there's more to business than just paying for your base salary. In fact, there are many business expenses in addition to your base salary that make up your total cost to your employer.

So Step 2 is to get yourself to a point where you're billing enough to pay for other expenses related to you, including payroll taxes, benefits, office space, and shared resources you use (physical devices like computers and printers, as well as human resources like secretaries, assistants, and accounting personnel). I've always thought of taxes and benefits as being worth at least an additional 20% on top of your salary, so assuming a salary of $50K, you need to be billing at least $60K per year to account for your taxes and benefits.

How you determine whether or not you're paying for the other resources depends on your particular circumstance. In my case I could easily account for the computer and human resources required to keep me rolling, but that may be harder for you. Suffice it to say that with a salary of $50K, I was pretty happy overall if I was billing at least $80K. I felt confident that I was at least breaking even for the company at that level. At that point I wasn't a burden to the company, and they could say that they could now handle Unix problems and C programming projects.

That may not sound like much, but just starting off the way I did, wow, those first eighteen months as a consultant were very lean times, and I constantly looked at these numbers to feel like I wouldn't be fired any time soon. But after those first eighteen months as a consultant I was easily generating over $100K in annual revenue for the company -- I was much closer to $200K per year -- and I knew my position in the firm was in good shape.

3) Get other people billing

Step 3 in my financial thought process was to get other people billing. Within my first thirty months as a consultant I had two other people working for me -- billing time to customers that I could easily prove to my supervisors was because of me. Not only that, I was indirectly billing a large number of people throughout the company, anywhere between an additional 1-5 people each week.

At this point I was extremely confident in my own success. I was getting a lot of other people to bill their time on my projects, and the money was rolling in. This can be a great time for you. It's nice to be able to go to the owners of the company and show them that you have your own "book of business" -- business you developed on your own, and business that is helping to pay existing employees, and hire new employees.

Step 0) Why the money was rolling in for me

When I said, "the money was rolling in," I meant that it was rolling in because I didn't ask for a flat salary of $50K when I came on board. In fact, I gave up a $50K/year job to join this firm, and we negotiated a deal that worked out great for everyone: I was paid a base salary of roughly $35K, and I was also paid a 10% "incentive" for any work that (a) I performed, (b) my employees performed, or (c) other people in the company performed on my projects.

As you can imagine, when you get a lot of people working for you at billing rates of $100/hour or more, yes, the money was rolling in for me. As money goes, I was happy, and management was happy. Financially, it was the first really good time of my life.

Summary

To summarize, my success formula for starting a career as a new consultant for an existing business followed these steps, most of which I didn't fully understand until after those first 36 months:

Step 0: Negotiate a good deal. In my case this was a low base salary with a 10% "incentive" on the work I generated throughout the company.

Steps 1, 2, and 3: As one of my managers liked to say, you "justify your existence" by billing more than the combination of your own salary plus benefits plus associated costs.

Step 4: Get other people working on your behalf. When more money is coming in the door, it's a good deal for everyone.

4.2) How I started a multimillion dollar consulting firm

*"When it's time to be a general, be a general.
When it's time to be a monk, be a monk."*

~ Unknown

A friend of mine is currently unemployed, and as I've talked to her about ways to approach her situation, I'm reminded of how I started Mission Data.

In the beginning, Mission Data was just me, Alvin Alexander. My wife became Employee #2, and she took care of the business and financial matters for me. After working like this for a while, I became interested in expanding the company, and in a chance meeting, I ran into a friend and former coworker, who was the best salesperson I ever knew. We ran into each other at a bookstore one night, and agreed to meet for lunch a few days later.

He wasn't happy with his current job, and I wanted to grow the company, so without knowing exactly what we did, or how to properly organize a company, he came on board. Our original slogan was "Data - Voice - Fax - [Something Else]" (I can't remember the last term), mostly because we had no idea what we did, and we were trying to keep every possible option open. The basic theory was that if you throw a bunch of crap on a wall, something will stick.

The business was run out of my basement, and my new business partner came over every day. We talked about different options, set up a phone system and network, and talked about who we knew. He began calling our old friends and coworkers, while I set up some additional infrastructure things, like a computer network and phone system.

Our first break

We finally got a break when he called a company I had worked with about five years earlier, where a friend of his was now working. The project I worked on with that company was successful in that we delivered a software application that did what we said it would do: It reduced the runtime of batch reports for advertising agencies from three days to less than three hours, while increasing the data set size by 300%.

Other than that, the project was a disaster: It was way over budget, and a little late. It was my first large project, I had no idea what I was doing, didn't know anything about Use Cases or software requirements, and was a relatively new C programmer. I gave my "methodology" the acronym "SLOP," which stood for Sheer Luck, Overtime, and Pain.

So, when this company agreed to take our phone call, and further agreed to an initial meeting, I was surprised.

The sales meeting

I went into the meeting expecting to meet with the people I had worked with previously, but to my further surprise, the company had gone through drastic changes, and we met with a person I didn't know, a man named Bill, who had recently been brought in as a VP to run the software group.

Bill was courteous enough, but the meeting just wasn't going well, and he was trying to show us the door. Finally, before we were kicked out, I blurted out, "How about this? I'll work for you for three days, free of charge. If you like my work, you can hire me if you'd like. If you don't like it, no hard feelings, you'll just have wasted a few resources on your part."

Bill thought about this for a few moments, and then for some reason he agreed to give me a chance.

Success

Fortunately it all went very well. The programmers I worked with were As/400 RPG developers who didn't know much about Java, but were eager to learn. I made a lot of progress, and to my surprise, on the second afternoon Bill gave us the account. Very shortly after this we hired a talented programmer we had been talking to, and the account served as a "pillar account," earning us over a millions dollars in the coming years.

That's the abridged story of how Mission Data, a consulting firm that would eventually grow to fifteen employees (and a few part-time contractors) was born. (I sold my interest in Mission Data in 2007, and used the sale of that business as the background for my book, *How I Sold My Business: A Personal Diary.*)

Summary

So, if you're a hard worker, but currently out of a job, or just interested in starting your own consulting company, I can tell you from my own experience, it can be done. As you can see, we didn't know anything magical, we just worked hard, and we didn't let what we didn't know stop us from doing what we wanted to do.

4.3) Being a good person is good business

*"The best way is to know the strict rules of karma,
and to work on our karma immediately."*

~ Zen Master Shunryu Suzuki

For anyone who knows me, I'm the high-paid consultant who accidentally unleashed a virus/worm on one of my customer's networks, and wreaked havoc on their business one day. To say the least, it wasn't one of the better days of my consulting life.

But more importantly, I'm also known as the consultant who (a) unleashed a virus/worm on my customer's network, and (b) continued to work for them for at least six more years, until I retired from the consulting world.

Surviving that event

How did I survive that horrible event? One word:

Goodwill

First, unlike many other consultants I've met, I'm not a jerk who thinks he's better than everyone else. I'd like to think that I'm a decent person to work with.

Second, once their network people showed me that my Windows laptop was Ground Zero for the worm being released on their network, I thought about the recent events of my laptop, and realized they were right. (I had to shut down my antivirus software to install an application, and unfortunately I forgot to turn it back on, and in less than an hour my Windows laptop was infected with this worm.) So in the midst of a room full of angry people who would just as soon kill me, I apologized, said they were right, and asked what I could do to help fix the problem. In my mind, once I knew the facts, this was the right thing to do.

Quote from "Growing a Business"

As I wrote those paragraphs I thought about one of my favorite quotes from my favorite business book, *Growing a Business*, by Paul Hawken:

> "Being a good person is good business."

In a way I've been lucky to work as a consultant in a midsize city (Louisville, Kentucky, 16th largest city in the United States). The area is small enough that many people in the IT community know each other, so if you're a consultant, sooner or later your reputation catches up with you.

Running into customers

I had a similar situation in 1995, after I left the first consulting firm I worked with. I left that firm because I didn't like the direction they were heading in. They seemed to value money and growth over quality, and they also had a tendency to treat customers roughly, especially if there was a question about money or a contract.

Just before I left that company in 1995, I was working with a regional telephone company, helping to set them up as an Internet Service Provider (ISP). When I was certain that the project was up and running, and in good hands with my client and my coworkers, I turned in my resignation at the consulting firm.

On our project there had been a dispute about something related to the contract, something that I was not involved in, but something that was making my sponsor more and more angry with our firm. (He was the CFO of the phone company.) Whatever that dispute was, I finished my project with the client and resigned before the two parties signed their contract. (I have no idea whether they ever had a signed agreement.)

While I felt okay with leaving the project at that time -- there wasn't much else for me to do personally -- I felt bad about this dispute.

And then a funny thing happened: Whenever I went out to eat lunch or dinner somewhere, the CFO of the phone company kept eating at the same restaurant. While I don't recall ever seeing him in public at any other time, we ran into each other at three straight restaurants. At the first two restaurants I politely waived to him, but didn't go to his table to say hello. I felt embarrassed by the contract situation with my former company.

But at our third meeting I finally went over and said hello to him, and as I apologized to him over the contract hassle with my former employer, he said, "Al, I'm not upset with you. I'm very upset with your former employer, but that has nothing to do with you. I'd gladly hire you again when we have the need."

At this point Mr. Hawken's quote that, "Being a good person is good business" really hit home.

4.4) Hire well

One of the most valuable lessons I learned when I created Mission Data was to hire well. Phrases like this have become more popular recently when people learned of the Steve Jobs quote, "A players hire A players, and B players hire C players," and other similar quotes. Guy Kawasaki, who was there during the early Apple days, expanded on this quote with his own thoughts:

> "My theory is that A players hire people even better than themselves. It's clear, though, that B players hire C players so they can feel superior to them, and C players hire D players. If you start hiring B players, expect what Steve called 'the bozo explosion' to happen in your organization."

Recognizing 'A' players

When I first moved to Kentucky and started working with a computer services firm there, I realized that out of the other twenty consultants they had at the company, only four of them were really good, people I would hire. I made a pact with myself that if I ever started my own company, I would only hire those people. Why?

As you can imagine, my first reason is that these people make problems go away. I looked at them as kindred spirits in that regard.

The second reason is that because they were so good, I could learn from them, and as a result, I looked forward to learning from them at every opportunity. They taught me about Novell, Microsoft, and computer networks, and I taught them about Unix and the internet.

Income at your own consulting firm

What makes this even better when you own your own consulting firm is that these people are *billing machines*. Customers love them, and you can lease them out at your highest billing rates. If a decent consultant just works a normal 2,000 hour work year, and you bill them out at $100/hour, that's $200,000 of revenue flow into your company. But if you can bill someone at $150/hour, that's $300,000 of revenue.

Adding *cost* numbers to those examples, if you pay the first consultant $90,000/year, and pay the second consultant $125,000/year, the first one nets you (the business owner) $110,000/year, but the other consultant nets you $175,000 per year!

As a final consideration, I haven't even discussed overtime here. It's been my experience that this second class of employees seems much more willing to work (and bill) overtime hours. In general, they are more driven and money-oriented people, which for you, the business owner, is a very good thing.

Not just money, but time

While those numbers are powerful on their own, the other thing to consider here is how much of *your* time each class of employee requires.

In the first case, you're probably paying the first consultant a little bit less because they're not quite as good as the other person. In my field, they weren't quite as good a programmer as the other people (they weren't as fast), or they weren't someone who could also run a project successfully. As a result, they required more assistance from other programmers, or they required more of my time to run their projects more successfully.

I know this is a cliche, but in the consulting field, where you bill for your time, it's especially true: Time is money. Looking at this from only my perspective, if I work a sixty-hour work week, I begin each

Monday knowing that my lesser employees will take up a certain amount of that week, let's say twenty hours, while the higher-paid employees will take up very little time, let's say two to four hours. That's a huge difference, and for our fifteen-person company, those numbers weren't an exaggeration. If you want to work fewer, happier hours, hire well.

Summary

Lesson learned: Hire self-sufficient people, give them what they need to succeed, you'll both make a lot of money, and your life as a business owner will be easier.

4.5) It takes a team

*"Things derive their being and nature by mutual dependence,
and are nothing in themselves."*

~ Nagarjuna

I mentioned earlier that when you're building a business, you should hire well, and this is true across every aspect of your business.

A "secret" that I stumbled onto when I started Mission Data is that you have to be strong everywhere: Marketing, sales, accounting, the service you provide, and you even need to have a good lawyer.

A service to sell

The first thing our company had was a service to sell, namely me. At that time I still worked on Unix systems, but I had also worked with three programming languages (C, Perl, and Java), and I wanted to get more into programming.

Handling the books

My wife took care of all the other things at the business, including acting as a receptionist, business manager, and handling all things related to bookkeeping (invoicing, payroll, etc.) and working with our accountant, so we were covered there.

A good salesperson

I mentioned that my first business partner was the best salesperson I knew when I hired him, and that's true. So we were fortunate, I could provide the initial services, and he could sell.

Whoops, we need marketing

Initially we had no marketing effort at all, it was just us calling on friends and old customers, but we very quickly knew we needed some sort of logo and a brand, and we'd also need someone who could help make good-looking websites. As luck would have it, this salesperson's wife was in charge of branding for a large business downtown, and for some reason she agreed to join us as well.

A complementary service - design

A funny thing is that although she had just joined our company, she helped us win one of our first large projects. A coworker and I put a lot of technical work into a demo to show our prospect what we could do, but our client seemed much more interested in how our web application looked, not how it worked, and if we hadn't brought her on to assure them that the application would look better than the demo, we might not have won that project.

More services to sell

Once she came on board, we were again fortunate to hire several very talented technical people who helped to make up for some of my weaknesses, and with everyone working well together, we suddenly had a pretty good team.

Wait, our lawyer sucks

As we grew the business, we needed to consult with a lawyer several times. This wasn't for lawsuits or anything like that, but just to make sure we had a good sales agreement, good employee agreements, and other small things like that. Our lawyer was always slow to respond to our needs, and despite us asking for the simplest possible legal documents, he kept sending us documents that were insanely obtuse, so we dumped him and found another lawyer specialized in the computer services field.

I, us, we

Throughout this book I often write "I" a lot when referring to my old company, but what I often mean is "us" or "we." I couldn't have done all the things we did together as team, and when you're starting a business, that gets back to the incredibly important point that you should hire well. No matter what department of our little business you looked at, we had good people doing good work, and we thrived as a result.

Lessons learned

Based on these early results, and later experiments, the simple lesson is, "hire well across all areas of your company."

Section 5: Your Career

At this point the pure "consulting" portion of this book has ended. As a bonus section to this book, I've included a collection of short stories that are related to your "career" in general.

Because I worked at least ten different jobs before graduating college, then started my career as an aerospace engineer, then switched to being a Unix Administrator, then a Programmer, and then a Programming Consultant, I've had the opportunity to see hundreds of work situations, and I've thought a lot about what I wanted in my career.

In this section I'll share a few notes on what I've learned about "Having a career." I'll again explore the topic of "attitude," and how it shapes your success, and also look at the employer/employee relationship.

5.1) What an employer looks for in an employee

"There is no 'try'."

~ Yoda

As a small business owner, I classify employees in three categories:

1. If employees have basic good qualities, I'd try to keep them through good times and bad.

2. If they were "problem" employees I got rid of them very quickly.

3. If employees had exceptional performance, they got the big raises, and I considered them as potential business partners.

Here's a quick look at those three categories.

1) The basic good qualities

At a very basic level, a "good" employee is someone with these attributes:

- They generally know how to do their job. (The level of supervision they need can vary depending on their experience.)

- They show up for work every day.

- There are no important problems with their personalities. In general they seem happy, and don't spread discontent. (They're not a "bad apple.")

- They seem to have a good work ethic, and will do what their boss asks of them.

If someone has these basic attributes, I'd consider them a decent employee, and they'll get good (if not great) raises.

2) Problem employees

On the other end of the spectrum there are the "problem employees." These employees have some of the following bad attributes that will get them fired, or will make them the first person to be laid off in a bad economy:

- Some part of their personality is a problem. They don't fit in, they're antisocial, constantly argumentative, they lead the gossip pool, they have a "can't-do, the sky is falling" attitude, etc.

- They don't give you an eight-hour workday. They either take a lot of breaks, spend a lot of time socializing, or sneaking around doing personal things that don't pertain to work while they're being paid to work, or have other issues in their personal lives.

- They don't know how to do their job, or get things done. I've fired several seemingly smart people who interview very well, but who just don't deliver work.

3) The employees who get big raises and promotions

My final list shows the attributes of employees that get better raises and promotions than everyone else:

- They have a positive, can-do, team-oriented personality and work ethic.

- They get their work done with little or no supervision.

- They proactively suggest ways to improve how things are done.

- They may be the best at what they do.

- They're capable of leading or managing other people.

In my opinion, people who are problem solvers, team players, and generally seem to be happy will always be able to find a job.

5.2) How much are you worth to your employer?

"He who knows others is wise.
He who knows himself is enlightened."

~ Lao-Tzu

A long time ago, around 1991, a friend of mine named Joe was a contractor for the aerospace company I worked at. Just like a consultant, Joe was paid by the hour.

At some point Joe decided he was going to leave that company to take a permanent job elsewhere, as he had a medical problem and wanted to get better insurance. Upon telling my employer of his plans, the employer came back and said, "What if we make you a full-time employee here?"

So they proceeded down the road to make Joe a full-time employee, but the process hit a snag. Because of his medical problem, my employer's insurance wouldn't pick him up.

At this point something really interesting happened. When Joe went back to talk to my employer about salary, he assumed he was talking about a *full-time* position, but the employer knew that the insurance company wouldn't pick Joe up, so they were talking about trying to keep him on as an hourly *contractor*.

So the employer asked, "Joe, how much would you like?", to which Joe only replied "80." (Like Clint Eastwood, Joe was a man of few words.) Fortunately for him he didn't say what he really meant, which was $80K per year.

Sitting on the other side of the table, the employer thought they were talking about a contracting rate, and they were stunned that he had the balls to ask for $80 per hour (remember, this was 1991), but since he was very good at what he did, they said, "We'll have to get back to you." Eventually they did get back to him -- giving him the $80 per hour they thought he asked for!

Yes, that's $160,000 in 1991 money for the 2,000 work-hours in a typical year, not to mention the extra pay for overtime we always pulled, which was up to 20 hours per week. Just working the math in my head, if you assume a cost of living increase of 4% per year, that "80" would be worth over $320,000 in salary in 2012 -- without considering the overtime! With the usual twenty hours per week of overtime we were working then, Joe would have made about $240,000 in 1991 -- a salary of nearly $500,000 per year in 2012 money.

Another story

I had a similar encounter with one of my exceptional employees. He was an indispensable employee, and one day he came to me in a very non-threatening manner with several facts. He knew (a) how many hours he billed in a year, (b) what we billed for his services ($125/hour, I think), and (c) what he was paid.

He came to me on this day with a spreadsheet, and again, very politely pointed out that he was being paid X, while based on these numbers, he thought he was worth Y, where 'Y' was a significantly larger number. We had a short discussion about the numbers, but frankly, I couldn't argue with him, he was right; he was worth more money to me. I didn't give him that new salary immediately, but because he was polite and factual in his approach, I gave him a higher salary soon thereafter.

A problem employee

While I hope those two stories show that if you're a good employee, you shouldn't be afraid to ask for what you're worth, I'd like to share another story.

In this story, another employee of mine thought it was a good idea to negotiate his salary several times a year. His approach was usually something like, "My friend over at Acme Corp is making $X. I think I should be making at least that." I found his approach threatening, and I also didn't like that he did this several times a year. I wouldn't have liked his approach this very much if he was a great employee, but in his case, he was only a very average performer. Replacing him would be simple, but he didn't see that.

I don't recall how many salary discussions we had, but I will say that the last one didn't go very well for him.

How much are you worth?

I think of these first two cases sometimes, and I wonder if good employees don't realize how much they're really worth to their employer. I know I paid my top-tier employees very, very well, and I'd like to think other good employers will do the same for their best employees.

5.3) The two things I learned in college

"The discipline of Zen consists in upsetting this groundwork once and for all, and reconstructing the old frame on an entirely new basis."

~ D.T. Suzuki

I was talking to a friend the other day about what I learned in college, and I came to the conclusion that I learned two major things.

1) Learning how to learn

First, I learned how to study, learn, and take tests. By throwing a lot of work at you, you're forced to learn a lot about how you learn. Some people learn things very naturally, and others, like me, have to go to other lengths to get things into our brains. For me, a terrific approach was to combine studying on my own along with studying with others at certain times, and I learned specific techniques that really helped me in both situations. (I found out that I learned best by writing things down with a pen and paper, talking about problems with friends, and using flashcards for memory-specific needs.) So without going into more detail on this topic, I learned how to learn.

2) Learn what the "game" is, and how to play it

Beyond this, the biggest thing I learned in college is that certain things in life – school life and business life – are a game. More importantly, if you're going to play these games and *win* these games you need to know what the rules are.

For instance, when I was at William Rainey Harper College in Illinois, I eventually got to be one of two people that could get A's on our lab reports in a very difficult Physics class. Actually, this lesson took two semesters. Despite a lot of work in my first semester (Physics 1), I got B's, and near the end of the semester I began wondering what the heck it would take to get A's. So I learned from the one person who did get the A's, and I modeled my work after his. (The teacher wanted his reports written in a particular style.) Then in the second semester (Physics 2) he and I were the only students to get A's on our lab reports. So out of a class that started with 34 students and ended up with only 13 students by the end of the second semester, I learned how to play the game and got the highest grade.

Is that the end of the story? No.

Next I went to Texas A&M University and took another class in the Aerospace Engineering Department that also required us to write lab reports. Of course I thought this was going to be easy, since I just beat everyone else and had a good formula for doing so: I'd just use that same formula here. So I did that, thought everything was great, and I got an 'F'. Fortunately almost everyone else also got an 'F', as the instructor was a maladjusted human being trying to teach us some type of lesson. I was pissed off, and everyone else was too.

What I learned from this maladjusted lab instructor was that I wasn't going to get a good grade unless I adjusted to him, because he certainly wasn't going to adjust to me (or anyone else in the class). I don't remember how I did this, but eventually I did, and began getting A's once again, and I never forgot this lesson.

The lesson

In summary, the lesson is simple:

> When someone is holding a grade over your head (the teacher in school) or is offering to give away large amounts of money (your employer or client), it's your responsibility to understand and adjust to what they want.

As a final point, you don't have to adjust, do you? You only have to adjust if you want to get the good grades, win the project, get the raise, etc. You do have the option of not adjusting – that's up to you. It just depends on whether you want to win "the game."

5.4) Conquering public speaking

"Practice your kicks 10,000 times."
~ From the book, "Dojo Wisdom for Writers"

"Breathing has an extremely important role in controlling thoughts."
~ Zen Master Shunryu Suzuki

You've seen in several sections of this book that being a great consultant involves being a great communicator. You need to be comfortable with public speaking, and you also need to be comfortable with speaking in sales situations and production meetings. Not only do you need to be comfortable with speaking, as you read in an earlier section, you need to be comfortable with influencing people.

If you're not comfortable with public speaking, you can do one of two things:

1. You can give up, as I almost did many years ago.

2. You can accept the fact that everyone is uncomfortable with public speaking at first, and get comfortable with it.

By getting comfortable with it, my salary rapidly increased from $50K/year to over $100K/year (in 1995 dollars), and my career became much more interesting. I'll leave the choice to you, but I highly recommend that you tackle your fear of public speaking head on.

Practice, practice, practice

My approach to conquering public speaking was to first rehearse in front of a mirror, then rehearse in front of coworkers.

Somewhere along the line I also started videotaping my rehearsals, which had a tendency to keep me on track and keep the pace moving just like I was in front of a crowd of people. At first, watching the recordings was brutal -- I was horrible! But over time I got better and better, removing all sorts of annoying habits I had while speaking, everything from rocking back and forth, to mumbling, and to using filler words like "um."

Between (a) this practice and (b) using my initial "flop sweat" presentation as motivation, my presentations eventually became good. I can't say they were "excellent," because I'm not the one to judge that, but they became good enough that I won some very large deals, and I'm now comfortable presenting in front of crowds of one hundred or more people.

As a final note, a friend of mine works in sales, and although he talks all the time in his role as a salesperson, he participates in a local speaking group known as Toastmasters. I've never been to one of their meetings, but as I understand it, the purpose of their meetings is to let everyone practice their public speaking skills in front of a friendly crowd. You prepare a small speech, present it in front of the group, and over time you become desensitized to speaking in front of crowds. Again, public speaking is your friend, and if you think it will help, I encourage you to join a group like this.

5.5) Career lessons from Project Runway

*"It takes a wise man to learn from his mistakes,
and an even wiser man to learn from others."*

~ Zen proverb

When I returned from Alaska in 2008, I lived with a friend for a little while, and she made me watch a TV show named *Project Runway*. She didn't really have to try too hard; I watched one episode with her, and I was hooked.

At first I enjoyed watching the show because I liked seeing the creativity of the contestants, but then the thing I really learned to enjoy was the *competition*.

Be open to competition

Can you imagine if all of your life was that competitive? I don't think I'd like that *all* the time, but I would like it some of the time, especially in business. I'd love to be on one team, competing openly against another. I know from my sports-playing days that competition does make you work harder, and in the case of this show, I thought it really improved the quality of the designs as the weeks went on.

When it comes to competition like this, these days I think, "Bring it on." I'll win some, and I'll lose some, but I'll also be better for it.

Work well in teams

The other thing I like about the show is that it reinforces something else for me:

> You can be a great *individual* designer, programmer, accountant, etc., but if you can't work well with other people, you're going to be limited in what you can achieve.

In some episodes of the show, they had the designers attempt to work together and compete as teams. For instance, if there were ten contestants, they'd split them into five teams of two, and those five teams would compete for the best design.

When they did this, you'd see that some designers who were very good by themselves were absolutely horrible teammates. Even though one person was designated as the team leader, the person who was supposed to be the "first mate" on the team just couldn't handle being in a support role. They couldn't handle not being the lead person, and they also couldn't have good discussions about designs. Instead of helping the lead person make their design better, they'd say something like, "If you had gone with my design we wouldn't have this problem."

I see this fairly often in the software world. If some programmers can't be the Lead Dog, they just don't participate well, they're not good teammates.

5.6) The karma of a pessimist

"You will not be punished for your anger.
You will be punished by your anger."

~ Buddha

As you can tell from this book, when I was young, I was a pessimistic person, but as I grew older, I worked hard to change my attitude into a positive, can-do person. If you think you can't change your attitude, I'm living experience that you can.

Pessimism is self-fulfilling

When you study Zen, you learn about this thing called "karma," and I believe it's true that pessimistic people bring problems onto themselves because of their attitudes. In one case, I met a person at a three-day seminar, and on the first morning our conversation went like this:

> Me: How was your hotel room last night?
> Other Person: Too loud, too cold, the bed was too hard.
> Me: Oh, I'm sorry to hear about that.
> Other: Well, what can you do?
>
> (later)
>
> Me: How was your breakfast? That stack of pancakes was enormous.
> Other: The coffee was cold, and I can make better pancakes.
> Me: Oh, I'm sorry to hear about that.
> Other: Well, what can you do?

After several more conversations like this throughout the first day, I thought to myself, "I know exactly what I can do: I'm not going to ask you any more questions."

In my experience, when all I get back from another person is negative feedback, I tend to quit talking to that person, or avoid them. I like to hang around with people who are fun, who help build me up, not bring me down.

More avoidance

If I'm stuck working with a pessimist, I'll try different approaches, including trying to pump up the pessimist with optimistic talk about how beautiful or cool everything is, what wonderful weather we're having, etc., but if it seems to have no effect, I'll quickly give up. It takes a lot of energy to try to pump up a person with a bad case of "Stinkin' Thinkin'".

I had this problem one time with a person who briefly visited with me in Alaska. Having lived in Alaska for over two years, I know many wonderful places to visit up there, but after getting a lot of negative vibes from this person on their first two days, I quit asking questions on the third day, and generally just stayed on the main road. There were beautiful spots just a few miles off the main roads that very few people knew about, but I just drove straight ahead without saying a word. "Shoot," I thought to myself, "I can see these spots next week, why bother taking this person there?" I had a "book on CD" in the car, so I just put that in, and we listened to it as I drove from one motel to the next.

Alaska is one of the most beautiful places in the world, and if you can't enjoy the outdoors here, wow, good luck to you. In addition to being a beautiful place, it's also a very expensive place to get to. By the simple act of being a buffoon, this person spent a lot of money, and saw very little.

The karma

As you can see from these examples, the karma of a pessimist is that the pessimist sets in motion a course of events where they see less in life, and thereby get less out of life. Beyond that, people avoid them, just like I've rarely seen this person again. I'm not an expert in psychology or even karma, but in my experience it seems like a pessimistic attitude leads to a self-fulfilling destiny where a pessimist may not do interesting things, and they may not have many friends.

In rural Alaskan communities there are dogs that just wander down the roads, and they look incredibly happy to just be alive. They wag their tails happily when they approach strangers, and love to be patted on the head. My advice is that if you approach your life like these dogs, and smile and seem happy just to be alive, you'll be amazed how many people will pat you on the head and give you something to eat. (They'll also take the time and effort to show you the coolest vacation spots in Alaska.)

This doesn't apply to work, does it?

If you think that being a pessimist isn't a self-fulfilling prophecy in your work life, think again.

A long time ago a coworker of mine had the same problem. Despite having a ton of energy and being a very sharp guy, he was always a pessimist. He would always tell our supervisor how hard something was, and that it couldn't be done the way he wanted. After a short while our supervisor quit asking him to do anything.

In the end -- even though this other person had as much talent as I did, or even more -- I did all the things that were "impossible," and he was let go. When I later started my own consulting business, this same company became one of my pillar clients, and we earned at least a million dollars in consulting fees from them.

After this other person I'm referring to was fired, he blamed this company for his problems, saying it was an impossible situation. He then went from one job to another, eventually quitting each job or being fired, and his attitude never changed. Along the way nobody ever told him the truth -- that his attitude was holding him back -- and each time he blamed the company he just left for his problems. (If I had known then what I know now, I would have taken him aside and talked to him, but I didn't know how to help him back then.)

5.7) "Excuse me, you're in my way"

By now you know that I think a lot about attitude, and if there are any major secrets to my success, one of them is that at some point I learned that I was smart enough, and aggressive enough, to know when I was right about something. Once I gained confidence in myself, if I was clearly right about something and someone didn't agree with me, I didn't hesitate to say, or at least think, "Excuse me, you're in my way."

Port covers

Just a few months out of college, I was assigned to a missile project that had to do with something known as "port covers." In short, port covers are like little doors on the sides of air-breathing rockets. If you've seen a little model rocket, or perhaps a firework that shoots up into the sky, you know that a rocket is basically a tube, like the cardboard tube that's inside a roll of toilet paper. A normal solid rocket motor like this is filled with solid rocket fuel, which is something like a solid version of gasoline.

With more advanced "air breathing" rocket motors, there are little doors on the sides of these tubes, and they open up after the solid fuel is burned off. On my project, these doors, which are hinged on one end just like a regular door, were called "port covers."

When these doors swing open, air from the outside is forced into the now-empty tube, which becomes a combustion chamber. Liquid fuel is injected into the tube, and the mixture of air and fuel is ignited, much like the combustion process that happens in your car engine.

A cheap cardboard model

I didn't really know too much about that when the project started, so I was nervous, and worked hard to try to understand what was going on. To help understand this, I had a coworker print off a CAD/CAM diagram that showed what everything looked like. One of the drawings he gave me showed what the system looked like if I could poke my head inside the end of the tube, and look straight down the middle.

Looking at the missile from this view, the outside of the tube looked like a simple circle. The diagrams he gave me were scaled down, so the tube happened to have a six inch diameter. In my struggle to understand everything, I got out a pair of scissors and cut this diagram up into different pieces. I pulled the cardboard back off the notebook on my desk, and created little cardboard port covers, pinning them on top of my six inch circle.

To my surprise, the port covers were much thicker than I expected. I said port covers are like doors, but they're really like curved doors, because on the outside they have to match the curved surface of the rocket. However, the inside of the port covers had to be reinforced to withstand the pressure, and as a result they were something like two inches thick, maybe a little thicker than that. In fact, the backs looked so deep, I went back to the CAD/CAM person to make sure this wasn't a mistake, but he said they were correct.

At this point, with my cardboard model in hand, it was obvious to me that there was a problem, but since the designer said in such a matter of fact way that everything was correct, I kept my mouth shut and walked away. I didn't want to look like the foolish young engineer I was.

But as I kept playing with my cardboard model, I could see that the port covers would interfere with each other. Because they were so deep, when one cover opened, it was almost impossible for the second cover to open. If the second cover failed to open, the system wouldn't get enough air, and the combustion chamber would have way too much fuel for the limited amount of air it was getting. The missile might explode, or otherwise fail to work.

The meeting

Still uncertain of what I was doing, I showed my model to the person I shared an office with. He said he knew nothing about it, but suggested I talked to a man named Ken, who was on the project, and was known for being both helpful and blunt.

By this time my first "big design meeting" was about to start, and as timing would have it, Ken had gone to the meeting early. Intent to talk to him before the meeting started, I hurried to the conference room, found him there, and began to show him what I was seeing.

As I started to show him what I was seeing, he began to laugh – at me, I thought! I had just ruined my career!

As I showed my model to Ken, several other engineers came into the meeting, saw my cardboard contraption, asked what it was, and as Ken told me to explain it, they also laughed. Several of them asked how much it cost, and with my career in ruins, I told them it was about $1.99 in materials, including the pins I borrowed from our secretary (now trying to poke fun at myself as well).

And then a funny thing happened. All the time I thought they were laughing at me, they were actually laughing at the problem: I was right!

Somehow a large contingent of high-paid engineers had missed the simple fact that the design couldn't possibly work. They were so busy working on other things, they hadn't noticed this problem. (I learned that the technical term for my discovery was "impingement.") The reason they asked about the cost was because they had already spent several hundred thousand dollars on the design, and I spent $1.99 to demonstrate that it wouldn't work.

A PhD and office politics

From a "political" standpoint I made one huge mistake here. By the sheer fact that I had just joined this company, straight out of college, and was just assigned to this project, this was my first big meeting. Because the meeting came on so fast, and I was struggling to get a grasp of the design, my cardboard model was created just before the meeting, and I had no time to run my findings past anyone before the meeting. I just wanted to show the model to Ken quietly, but because I was right and he was a no-BS guy, he (and I) shared the finding with everyone else.

The part where my finding becomes a problem is that I destroyed the meeting of a young PhD who was seen as someone climbing the corporate ladder. I was later told he always came to his own meetings late, and as a result of this behavior, everyone on the project knew about this problem before he did. In fact, other engineers were called to this meeting when Ken and I demonstrated my model, so even those people knew about the problem before this PhD did. While all these engineers put away their own pre-planned notes to focus on the logical discussion of, "Where do we go from here?", this PhD wasn't even at his own meeting yet.

When he finally came in, Ken demonstrated my device, and while all the engineers had another good laugh, the PhD's face turned red and he glared at me. I had made him look bad, very bad.

I was oblivious to corporate politics at that time, but my supervisor, who wasn't at that meeting, later told me that this PhD was a "political animal," and that although I was right, and had probably saved the company hundreds of thousands of dollars, I had committed a breach of etiquette. Because the PhD was intent on climbing the corporate ladder, I had probably just made an enemy of him for a long time to come.

"Bite Me"

This experience – and several experiences after this – taught me that there are times in life when you just have to say, "Excuse me, you're in my way." Or, as one of my sisters likes to say, "Bite me."

What I mean by this is that you have to be confident enough in your abilities, so that when you know you're right and someone else is wrong, you can stand your ground, no matter who that other person is. I didn't do it then, but if the same situation came up now, I'd talk to the PhD after the meeting, explain to him what happened, and help him see that I/we had just saved the project hundreds of thousands of dollars. (It takes a *lot* of money to build a rocket motor and test it. You're much better to find problems like this in the design phase.)

Beyond that, I'd probably tell him that in the future I'll come to him with problems like this, and also remind him that he's probably much better off that I'm on his team.

Unfortunately it didn't work out that way back then, and this PhD rarely spoke to me after this meeting. After this experience I learned to say, or at least think, "We're supposed to be on a team together, and if you're that worried about how you look instead of building a successful product and making our company successful, excuse me, you're in my way."

If you're concerned about office politics you should be careful about how you handle these situations, but this is where I can appreciate a leader like Steve Jobs, who was open to confrontation.

The best idea wins

Another way to look at this situation is what the famous physicist Richard Feynman once wrote:

> "The best idea wins."

I remember reading this quote in one of his books where he was talking about the building of the atomic bomb, and how Neils Bohr and his son would seek out the very young Feynman at that time. Bohr felt that many of the other top scientists were "Yes" men who would only agree with Bohr, while Feynman was young and I, and would just tell Bohr what he thought.

What Feynman meant by this phrase is that you have to be able to have good, hard conversations with people about important topics, and at the end of the day you have to put your ego aside, and the team should go forward with the best idea, no matter where it came from.

Hold your ground

Another example of this attitude is when I bought a car a few years ago. I've always owned red cars, and in this case I wanted a red Toyota RAV4. So I went to a Toyota dealer, met a salesperson, and said, "I want to trade in my current car, and I want $6,500 for it, and I want to buy a red RAV4 with these specs, and I'm willing to pay $19,000 for it."

"We don't have a red RAV4 in stock, but I have a silver one or black one I can show you, and ..." he started to say.

"No thank you, I want a red RAV4," I said.

"But we don't have any of those in stock, it will cost more ..."

"No it won't," I said, apparently using a Jedi mind trick, "I'm willing to pay $19,000 for these specs for a red RAV4."

The whole sale took less than two hours. I was polite but persistent throughout the discussion, and got what I wanted. My red RAV4 was delivered to the dealership two days later.

As we signed the paperwork, the salesperson told me he was stunned at my persistence, and wouldn't normally order a different car for someone just because they wanted a red one, he'd find a way to sell them one off the lot. I told him it never occurred to me that he wouldn't do that; I came to buy a red car, and I'd have it no other way.

When people are too nice

One other place where I've found that having the same attitude of persistence, determination, and doing the right thing is when the people you're working with are moving too slow.

I had this happen one time when I was working on a project with a large religious organization. It turns out that the people there were so nice that none of them wanted to contradict each other, or state anything with any certainty. They were *too* nice, and didn't want to hurt each other's feelings, and as a result, nothing ever got done.

It would have been nice to know about this problem going into our project – we would have raised our estimate for the project! But as my team started to see this behavior, we realized that if it didn't change, we would soon be over budget. So we essentially took the same tact that I've mentioned in this chapter and others. We told our project sponsor (the person who hired us) about this problem, and working with him, we quit asking what everyone thought, made decisions for them, and gave them our best advice, as though they were our brothers, sisters, or best friends.

In this example, I had a more pleasant experience of the thought, "Excuse me, you're in my way." I wasn't upset with anyone on the project, they were nice and thoughtful people, but I needed to get the project completed on time and within budget, and this was the only way we could do it.

One important note here: This technique only worked because our project sponsor knew about the problem, and also thought it was important for us to stay on time and within budget. I've worked on other projects where I didn't have this same support from the project sponsor, and that's a much more difficult situation.

Summary

Again, my reasons for these stories are simple; I'm trying to share stories about my attitude. In this case of the red RAV4, if you know what you want, go out and get it, and don't let anyone change your mind.

In the story of working with the polite religious organization or the earlier port cover story, if someone is in your way, politely say or think, "Excuse me, I'm going somewhere, and you're in my way." (Or, as my sister likes to say, "Bite me.")

In all of these stories, I tried to act like a guided missile, or a football player trying as hard as possible to get the ball in the end zone. I was determined to get that goal, and go through any obstacles that were in my way. Looking at these situations now, I can see that my important attributes were being persistent and determined, while also trying to do the right thing.

5.8) All you are is attitude

"You must concentrate upon and consecrate yourself wholly to each day, as though a fire were raging in your hair."

~ Taisen Deshimaru

Your attitude is such an important topic, I want to end this book by getting you to look at yourself the way other people see you.

Technical twins

First, put yourself in the position of a person that needs to hire someone who offers whatever service you offer (programmer, designer, etc.). Completely imagine that you are this person, The Buyer. For instance, I design software systems, and I usually sell my services to other IT people, so I'll put myself in the shoes of an IT Manager or Project Manager who needs an architect like myself.

Putting myself in their shoes, I have a good feel for all the technical skills an architect needs. After I do my legwork and interview many architects, I eventually end up with two primary candidates. Their technical skill sets are so good and so close I can't tell the difference between them -- they're technical twins!

Yes, they are *technical* twins, but as I think about them, they're not *emotional* twins. In fact, there are some major differences:

Person A seems a little tired, disorganized, takes a deep sigh every time I start to ask another question, and they seem to have the attention span of a gnat.

On the other hand, Person B seems enthusiastic, interested in my problems, organized, and a real problem-solver.

Hopefully you'll agree that all technical considerations being equal, Person B is the one you'd hire. (Taking this a little farther, I suspect you'd hire Person B even if they didn't seem quite as talented as Person A.)

Look at yourself

Your next task is to take an honest look at yourself, and ask, "How do I come across to other people? Am I more like Person A, or Person B?"

Don't lie to yourself -- be honest here. You don't have to be perfect. Nobody is perfect all the time. Heck, if we were, life would be really boring, wouldn't it? But if you tend to be a lot more like Person A than Person B, this could be a big reason why you're not landing the big accounts or getting the promotions.

It may be that you're a very nervous person, and you're letting your nervousness get the best of you, and so you come across as Person A. Or, it could be that you don't like your job, or you're burned out, and you need some time off, or a serious change of scenery. In any case, if you're coming across as Person A, I think you can understand why people aren't hiring you: Getting hired is a competition, and you have to learn to compete well.

Ask other people

You get into dangerous territory when you ask other people to give you an honest assessment of your personality, because if you can't handle it, it can end your friendship. With that being said, if you can't assess yourself honestly, and you can really handle the truth, talk to friends or relatives, people you trust, and ask them to give an honest assessment of your personality.

Ask them about all of the qualities I've written about in this book, things like honesty, trustworthiness, enthusiasm, happiness, and having a can-do attitude, and a history of getting things done. Ask them to rate these attributes on a scale of one to ten, and ask them for specific instances of things you've done well, and things you've handled poorly.

Again, I caution you that this can ruin your relationship with this person, so before going down this road, I encourage you to assess yourself. Think about how you might be weak in each attribute, and make a definite plan to eliminate your weaknesses.

In my case, I knew I had to take this approach, because I knew that if I didn't, I would have lived a life filled with regret, and I just couldn't let that happen.

If you really take the time and effort to do this, the income you receive in your lifetime may be many hundreds of thousands of dollars higher over your lifetime -- maybe even millions -- and your work will be much more rewarding and fun.

How I raised myself from failure to success

Assuming that (a) you don't really hate what you do for a living, and (b) you're not burned out, I highly recommend reading the book "How I Raised Myself from Failure to Success in Selling," by Frank Bettger. I have a 1949 version of this book (wow, over 60 years old!), which I was fortunate enough to receive from my wife's grandfather. Although the book is mostly about selling, it's also about human nature, and how to change your own nature for the better. The first chapter on enthusiasm is worth the price of the book many, many times over.

In that chapter Mr. Bettger writes about being nervous, and how that nervousness used to hold him back, until he learned to channel his nervous energy into enthusiasm. I had the exact same problem, and that first chapter was a life-changer for me. I just re-read it now, and it still gets me fired up.

In another important chapter on life, Mr. Bettger writes about Benjamin Franklin, and the struggles Mr. Franklin had with his own caustic personality, and the steps he went through to become much less abrasive, eventually becoming the great statesman he's known for being today. Just like the first chapter, this chapter is again well worth the price of admission. (I've written about Mr. Franklin's technique in the chapter titled, "Who do you buy from?")

A little card in my wallet

Until rereading that chapter just now, I had forgotten that for years I walked around with a simple little card in my wallet, a card that I made myself, in part based on this book by Mr. Bettger. On that card I wrote one little statement:

I will be the most positive and enthusiastic person I meet today.

Several times a day, especially when things were at their worst, I'd pull that card out and read it to myself over and over again. I can specifically recall sitting in a bathroom stall during one of my most difficult projects, and reading that card repeatedly. That project was full of all sorts of obstacles, and I firmly believe that card was the only thing that got me through it.

To be clear on this point, I attribute hundreds of thousands of dollars of my own personal income to Mr. Bettger's book, and to this card I created. By reading his book, using Ben Franklin's technique, and constantly referring to this card, I changed my attitude, my approach to business, and my approach to other people.

The 80% rule

I don't know the exact numbers, but I think it's correct to say that 80% of people are either fired, or not hired, because of nontechnical reasons. When I say, "nontechnical," I'm being polite. What that really means is "because of personality issues."

I won't go into any personal stories that I had with employees, but I have to agree with this statement. If you count "inability to finish a project" as a personality problem and not a technical problem, I can't think of anyone I've ever fired for purely technical reasons.

Summary

In closing, I highly recommend that you work your butt off to cultivate the following personality traits:

1. Be an honest person, with others, and with yourself.

2. Be the most enthusiastic person you know.

3. Approach each day with a positive, can-do, problem-solver attitude.

If you'll strive for just those traits alone, I believe you'll find your income will go through the roof, just as mine did.

Summary Guides

This section provides a summary of the first four sections of this book (Consulting, Sales, Marketing, and Your Business). I hope it will be a helpful reference for you.

Summary: Consulting

Where there's mystery, there's money

Customers generally pay you because you know something they don't know, there's a "mystery" aspect to your work. The more the mystery, the higher your billing rate.

Rule #1: Deserve trust

Be honest, and deserve trust.

Rule #2: Be a problem solver

Become something like a "technical hit man," and make problems go away.

Keep the peace

When working at client sites, don't create problems for your sponsor. Make them look great for bringing you in.

If you were my brother ... giving advice

When giving advice, have complete empathy for your client. Envision them as being your brother, sister, or best friend.

Influencing people

You influence people by knowing what you want to say, and then saying it in a straightforward, problem-solving manner. Like controlling buffalo, you show them a big, green, happy pasture.

Running a great meeting

The simple secret to running a great meeting is to know exactly what you want out of the meeting, long before the meeting begins.

You can't always save the client

No matter how good you are, you can't always save the client. There may be hidden or political issues that you won't be able to overcome, but hopefully these situations are rare.

Other tips

Become a great listener. "Seek first to understand, then be understood."

Learn to assess people quickly.

Under-promise and over-deliver (not the other way around).

Don't waste time.

Summary: Sales

Who do you buy from?

We buy from people we trust who are enthusiastic about their product.

Be a "Buyer's Assistant"

Envision yourself as an assistant buyer for your prospect, and act in their best interests.

Tell your story

In sales meetings you'll have an opportunity to tell your story. As with any public speaking, be prepared so you can say it easily.

Ask questions

Ask questions during the sales process, and let the prospect sell themselves on your service.

Be ready for battle

Be prepared to handle objections. For hidden objections, ask, "In addition to that ..."

If you just don't like selling

First, know that you're always selling something. Second, think of the process as being a Buyer's Assistant. Third, you're selling your own skills; what would you rather sell?

Contractual matters

Get sales agreements and other legal documents from your lawyer, and keep them simple.

More sales tips

See the people. Keep records of how many people you attempt to sell to. At the very least, selling is a numbers game.

Be enthusiastic. As Mr. Bettger writes, enthusiasm is probably the single most important attribute to selling.

Assume the sale. Expect that you'll make the sale, have a contract prepared and ready for signature, and give the client the contract and a pen.

Summary: Marketing

Your best advertising

Your best form of advertising is existing clients. Ask for referrals, and ask if they have other projects you can help with.

Your second-best form of advertising

Find great ways to get prospects to meet you.

Make your phone ring

Cold-calling is bad, and getting customers to come to you is good.

How to sell your service

Find ways to package your service as a product so it becomes more tangible. Create a portfolio of your work, or something similar.

Sell the sizzle, not the steak

Sell emotions, not facts.

What's your brand?

Your brand is how people think about your company, product, or service. Make sure everything you do reflects your brand, including your marketing, sales approach, and service.

Who are your customers?

Don't waste time trying to market to people who won't buy your service. Know your target customers, and market to them exclusively.

Networking

Find networking events where you can meet your target customers. Learn how to introduce yourself and keep a conversation moving.

Summary: Building a Consulting Business

How I started my consulting career

When I started my career I had no idea what I was doing. Review this chapter and learn as I did.

Hire well

Hire great people, make more money, and work will be easier.

Being a good person is good business

When you let a virus/worm loose on your client's computer network, it's really helpful if you otherwise have trust and goodwill in your favor.

Build a great team

When you start your business, you want to be strong in sales, marketing, accounting, as well as the service you provide. Any weakness will cause problems.

Your Notes

This space is intentionally left blank so you can add your own notes, to help make this book your own.

Recommended Reading

After I sold Mission Data in 2007, I also sold most of my belongings and drove to Alaska, a state I fell in love with during several vacations many years ago. As a result of that moving process, I sold over 400 books, keeping only the 100 or so "best" books that would fit in my car.

Forced to think about keeping only ~100 books, I learned that my favorite business books are:

1. How I Raised Myself From Failure to Success in Selling, by Frank Bettger

2. Growing a Business, by Paul Hawken

3. Selling Your Services, by Robert Bly

As I've mentioned throughout this book, the first book by Mr. Bettger helped change my life, and I recommend it highly.

Shore up your weaknesses

Beyond these books, I encourage you to read any book that will help you shore up an area of weakness. For instance, for many years I didn't know anything about investing in stocks, so I bought several books and then began investing on my own. Everything related to this experience helped me talk to CEO's and small business owners, as these people also commonly invest in the stock market.

Similarly, I was trained as an engineer, and when I got into the software business I learned that designers think *very* differently than engineers. I also learned that to be successful, software needs to look as good as it works, so I bought several books related to design -- and I'm a better consultant as a result.

Zen quotes

The Zen quotes used in this book come primarily from the following books:

1. Zen Mind, Beginner's Mind, by Shunryu Suzuki

2. Only Don't Know, by Zen Master Seung Sahn

3. The Teachings of Don Juan: A Yaqui Way of Knowledge, by Carlos Castaneda

4. Zen Training, by Katsuki Sekida

5. Tao Te Ching, by Lao Tzu

More Information

As I finish editing this book in January, 2014, it's a busy time. In addition to releasing this book, I just finished writing a 700+ page computer programming book for O'Reilly named *Scala Cookbook*.

If you're interested in contacting me, you can reach me in a variety of ways:

- My alvinalexander.com website
- My OneMansAlaska.com website
- My Twitter account: https://twitter.com/alvinalexander

I offer my consulting services through my company in Boulder, Colorado:

- Valley Programming: valleyprogramming.com

I also started a nonprofit, charitable organization to help make Zen books freely available:

- The Zen Foundation: zenfoundation.org

As I mentioned a few times in this book, I've also written another book named, *How I Sold My Business: A Personal Diary*. It's currently available on Amazon.com as an eBook.

I hope you have enjoyed reading this book, and even more importantly, I hope it will help you find wealth and happiness in your career!

All the best,
Alvin Alexander

Made in the USA
San Bernardino, CA
01 October 2014